Travel

MW00898298

Angkor Wat, Cambodia

Nature's Escape in the City: Your Guide to Angkor Wat, Cambodia Hidden Gems

Julie Moore

TABLE OF CONTENTS

Chapter 4: Accommodation

4.1 Overview of Accommodation Options.

Selecting the Right Accommodation for You

Booking Tips and Tricks

3. Consider Local Homestays:

4.2 Luxury Resorts

2. Belmond La Résidence D'Angkor

4. Raffles Grand Hotel d'Angkor

4.3 Budget-Friendly Hotels

1. Green Valley Guesthouse

Location:

2. Rosy Guesthouse

Location:

3. Onederz Cambodia.

Location:

4. The Rose Apple Bed and Breakfast

4.4 Boutique Guesthouses

2. Jaya House River Park

Chapter 1: Introduction

Welcome to Angkor Wat, a mesmerizing destination that beckons you with its rich history and cultural treasures. Nestled in the heart of Cambodia, Angkor Wat is not just a temple; it's a living testament to the ancient Khmer civilization and a UNESCO World Heritage Site that draws the hearts of hundreds of millions of visitors every year.

Brief History and Cultural Significance

Dating back to the 12th century, Angkor Wat stands as the largest religious monument globally, a symbol of the Khmer Empire's architectural brilliance. Originally constructed as a Hindu temple dedicated to the god Vishnu, it later transformed into a Buddhist temple. The intricate carvings on the temple walls depict epic tales of mythology and history, showcasing the mastery of the Khmer artisans.

Beyond Angkor Wat's walls, the entire Angkor Archaeological Park unfolds, revealing a city of temples, ancient reservoirs, and forgotten structures. Each edifice narrates a unique story, from the enigmatic faces of Bayon Temple to the entwined roots of Ta Prohm, echoing with the whispers of centuries past.

The cultural significance of Angkor Wat extends beyond its historical roots. It remains a sacred site for Buddhists, attracting pilgrims who seek spiritual solace amidst its serene surroundings. The temple complex also plays host to traditional ceremonies, offering visitors a glimpse into Cambodia's vibrant cultural tapestry.

Dos and Don'ts for a Respectful Visit

As you embark on your Angkor Wat adventure, it's crucial to embrace a respectful approach to ensure a harmonious experience:

Dos:

1. Dress Appropriately: Wear modest clothing that covers your shoulders and knees. This demonstrates respect for the site's historical and cultural heritage.

2. Follow Guided Tours: Engage with knowledgeable local guides who can provide historical context and enrich your understanding of Angkor Wat.

3. Silence and Reverence: Maintain a quiet demeanor within the temple premises, allowing others to immerse themselves in the spiritual ambiance.

4. Remove Hats and Shoes: As a sign of respect, remove your hat and shoes before entering temple buildings.

5. Support Local Communities: Contribute to the preservation of the site by purchasing souvenirs from local artisans and supporting community-based initiatives.

Don'ts:

1. Disruptive Behavior: Avoid loud conversations, music, or disruptive behavior that may disturb the tranquility of the sacred space.

2. Touching Carvings: Refrain from touching the ancient carvings, as oils from the skin can contribute to deterioration.

3. Unauthorized Climbing: Climbing on temple structures is strictly prohibited to prevent damage and ensure visitor safety.

4. Littering: Keep the site pristine by disposing of waste in designated bins. Littering is both disrespectful and harmful to the environment.

5. Commercial Photography: Respect the rules regarding commercial photography to protect the sanctity of the site.

In summary, a visit to Angkor Wat is not just a sightseeing venture; it's an immersive cultural experience. By adhering to these dos and don'ts, you contribute to the preservation of this extraordinary heritage site and foster a positive interaction between visitors and the local community.

Welcome to Angkor Wat – where history, spirituality, and culture converge to create an unforgettable journey.

Chapter 2: Getting Started

2.1 Planning Your Trip

Embarking on a journey to Angkor Wat requires thoughtful planning to ensure a seamless and enriching experience. Let's delve into essential details to get you started on this captivating adventure.

Best Time to Visit

The climate in Cambodia greatly influences the ideal time to visit Angkor Wat. The months between November and March constitute the dry season, characterized by cooler temperatures and clear skies. This period is particularly favorable for exploring the temples, as the weather is more comfortable, and the landscapes are lush from the preceding rainy season.

On the other hand, the wet season, spanning from May to October, brings occasional heavy rainfall. While this season may deter some travelers, it offers a unique perspective of Angkor Wat surrounded by vibrant greenery and fewer crowds. Keep in mind that some temple areas might be inaccessible due to flooding during this time.

Entry Requirements and Visa Information

Before embarking on your journey, familiarize yourself with Cambodia's entry requirements. Most visitors are required to obtain a visa to enter the country. Fortunately, the process is straightforward. You can obtain a visa on arrival at major entry points or apply for an e-visa online before your trip.

Ensure your passport is valid for at least six months beyond your planned departure date and that you have a few passport-sized photos for visa applications.

Packing Essentials for a Trip to Angkor Wat

Packing thoughtfully can significantly enhance your Angkor Wat experience. Here's a comprehensive list of essentials to ensure you're well-prepared for your visit:

1. Comfortable Clothing: As Angkor Wat is a religious site, it's essential to dress modestly. Lightweight, breathable clothing that covers shoulders and knees is recommended. A hat and sunglasses for sun protection are also advisable.

2. Comfortable Footwear: Expect to do a fair amount of walking, so comfortable, closed shoes are crucial. Sandals or sneakers are ideal for navigating temple grounds.

3. Weather-Appropriate Gear: Depending on the season, pack a rain jacket and an umbrella for the wet season. In the dry season, sunscreen and a reusable water bottle are must-haves.

4. Daypack: A small backpack to carry your essentials, including water, snacks, sunscreen, and your camera, is practical for exploring the vast temple complex.

5. Electronics and Photography Gear: Don't forget your camera or smartphone for capturing the breathtaking scenery. Ensure you have sufficient storage and battery life.

6. Travel Adapters: Cambodia typically uses Type A, C, or G electrical outlets, so bring suitable travel adapters to charge your devices.

7. Health Essentials: Pack a basic first aid kit with essentials like pain relievers, insect repellent, and any personal medications you may need.

8. Guidebook or Maps: While guided tours are available, having a guidebook or map can enhance your understanding of the temples' history and layout.

9. Cash and Cards: While major tourist areas may accept credit cards, it's wise to carry some local currency for small purchases and markets.

10. Respectful Accessories: A sarong or scarf can be useful to cover shoulders when necessary and can also serve as a respectful accessory during temple visits.

By planning your trip meticulously, considering the best time to visit, understanding entry requirements, and packing the essentials, you set the foundation for an enjoyable and stress-free exploration of the wonders of Angkor Wat. As you prepare for your journey, remember that the key to a fulfilling visit lies inimmersing yourself in the rich culture and history that this UNESCO World Heritage Site has to offer.

2.2 Budgeting and Money Matters

Navigating Angkor Wat on a budget doesn't mean sacrificing the awe-inspiring experience that this historical marvel promises. Let's break down budgeting and money matters, providing insights to make your visit both economical and memorable.

Cost Estimates for Different Travel Styles

Budget Traveler:

Accommodation: Budget-friendly guesthouses and hostels in Siem Reap start at approximately $15-30 per night. Opt for local eateries, where meals can cost as little as $2-5. Tuk-tuks, a popular mode of transportation, are reasonably priced for short distances.

Entrance Fees: The Angkor Pass, granting access to the entire archaeological park, costs $37 for a one-day visit, $62 for three days, and $72 for a week. For budget travelers, a one-day pass provides a comprehensive glimpse.

Mid-Range Traveler:

Accommodation: Comfortable mid-range hotels and boutique stays are available from $40-150 per night. These options often include additional amenities such as pools and complimentary breakfasts.

Dining: Enjoy a mix of local and international cuisine at mid-range restaurants, with meals costing between $10-20. Consider sampling traditional Khmer dishes for an authentic experience.

Transportation: Tuk-tuks and taxis are readily available. Consider hiring a tuk-tuk driver for a day, costing around $20-30, to explore the temples at your own pace.

Luxury Traveler:

Accommodation: Indulge in luxury resorts surrounding Angkor Wat, with prices ranging from $200-800 per night. Experience opulent amenities, exquisite dining, and impeccable service.

Dining: Fine dining establishments within luxury resorts or high-end restaurants in Siem Reap offer diverse culinary experiences, with meals averaging $30-100.

Private Tours: Engage in private guided tours for a personalized exploration of Angkor Wat and its surrounding temples. Prices vary but can range from $100-500 per day.

Currency Exchange Tips

Understanding currency exchange is vital for managing expenses effectively in Cambodia. The Cambodian Riel (KHR) is the official currency, while US dollars are often accepted.

Currency Exchange Tips:

1. Carry US Dollars: While Riel is the official currency, US dollars are commonly used for larger transactions, such as accommodation and entrance fees. Ensure bills are clean and unmarked for wider acceptance.

2. Use Local Currency for Small Purchases: For small purchases like street food and souvenirs, it's advisable to use Riel. This helps avoid unfavorable exchange rates and simplifies transactions.

3. Exchange Money at Reliable Places: Choose authorized money changers or banks for currency exchange. Be cautious with street money changers, and always count your money before leaving.

4. ATMs in Siem Reap: ATMs are widely available in Siem Reap, dispensing both US dollars and Riel. Notify your bank of your travel plans to avoid any issues with your card.

Managing Expenses Effectively

Accommodation Options:

1. Budget-Friendly: Consider guesthouses like Rosy Guesthouse or Green Valley Guesthouse, starting at $15 per night.

2. Mid-Range: Explore options like Tara Angkor Hotel or Viroth's Hotel, ranging from $40-100 per night.

3. Luxury Stays: Indulge in the grandeur of resorts like Belmond La Résidence d'Angkor or Phum Baitang, starting from $200 per night.

Dining Tips:

1. Street Food: Savor affordable local delights from street vendors. Try dishes like Khmer noodles or grilled skewers for a genuine culinary experience.

2. Local Markets: Visit Pub Street Night Market for budget-friendly meals and souvenirs. Haggle for better prices while respecting local sellers.

3. Set Menu Options: Many restaurants offer set menu options, providing a variety of dishes at a fixed price.

Transportation:

1. Tuk-Tuks: A cost-effective and iconic mode of transport. Negotiate prices before setting off, and agree on a daily rate if exploring multiple temples.

2. Bicycles: Renting bicycles is a budget-friendly and eco-friendly way to explore the temples. Daily rates are around $2-5.

3. Guided Tours: If opting for a guided tour, compare prices and read reviews. Many agencies offer affordable group tours.

Miscellaneous Expenses:

1. Entrance Fees: Plan your temple visits strategically to make the most of your purchased Angkor Pass.

2. Souvenirs: Bargain at local markets and choose souvenirs wisely. Handicrafts and traditional textiles are popular choices.

3. Tipping: While not mandatory, tipping is appreciated. Round up taxi fares or leave a small tip at restaurants if service isn't included.

In conclusion, exploring Angkor Wat on a budget is not only achievable but can also enhance your cultural immersion. By considering cost estimates for different travel styles, understanding currency exchange tips, and managing expenses effectively, you pave the way for a rewarding and economical adventure in this remarkable destination.

Chapter 3: Itineraries and Sample Plans

3.1 Weekend Getaway

Embarking on a weekend getaway to Angkor Wat is an enticing prospect, offering a glimpse into the captivating world of ancient temples and rich history. Here, we present quick highlights for a short trip and a meticulously crafted 2-day itinerary for a weekend escape.

Quick Highlights for a Short Trip

Day 1: Arrival and Sunset at Angkor Wat

Morning:

Arrive in Siem Reap and check into your chosen accommodation.

Enjoy a quick breakfast at a nearby local eatery.

Afternoon:

Begin your temple exploration with a visit to Angkor Thom, marveling at the grandeur of Bayon Temple.

Have lunch at a nearby restaurant, savoring Khmer cuisine.

Evening:

Explore the Terrace of the Elephants and the mysterious Ta Prohm temple.

Conclude your day with a mesmerizing sunset view at Angkor Wat.

Day 2: Sunrise at Banteay Srei and Floating Village

Early Morning:

Catch the sunrise at the intricately carved Banteay Srei temple.

Have breakfast on the way back to Siem Reap.

Late Morning:

Visit the Angkor National Museum for a deeper understanding of Khmer history.

Explore local markets like Old Market and Pub Street for unique souvenirs.

Afternoon:

Enjoy a relaxing lunch in Siem Reap.

Take a tuk-tuk ride to the fascinating floating village of Kampong Phluk.

Evening:

Return to Siem Reap for dinner and explore the vibrant nightlife on Pub Street.

2-Day Itinerary for a Weekend Escape

Day 1: Temple Immersion

Morning:

Start your day early with a visit to Angkor Wat to witness the sunrise, a breathtaking spectacle.

Explore the intricate bas-reliefs and galleries of Angkor Wat.

Late Morning:

Head to Bayon Temple in Angkor Thom, known for its iconic smiling faces.

Visit the Terrace of the Elephants and the Terrace of the Leper King.

Afternoon:

Enjoy lunch at a local restaurant.

Explore the jungle-covered Ta Prohm, famous for its intertwining tree roots.

Evening:

Conclude your day with a visit to Phnom Bakheng for panoramic sunset views.

Day 2: Hidden Gems and Cultural Insights

Early Morning:

Discover the pink sandstone temple, Banteay Srei, renowned for its delicate carvings.

Breakfast at a nearby café.

Late Morning:

Visit the Angkor National Museum for a comprehensive overview of Khmer civilization.

Explore the lesser-known Preah Khan temple.

Afternoon:

Enjoy a leisurely lunch in Siem Reap.

Take a tuk-tuk ride to the captivating floating village of Kampong Phluk.

Evening:

Return to Siem Reap for dinner, exploring the bustling Pub Street and its vibrant night market.

This 2-day itinerary offers a perfect balance of iconic temples, hidden gems, and cultural insights, ensuring you make the most of your weekend getaway to Angkor Wat. Customize your experience based on personal preferences and interests, and immerse yourself in the wonders of this UNESCO World Heritage Site.

3.2 Cultural Immersion

Immerse yourself in the rich cultural tapestry of Angkor Wat, where every temple tells a story, and every carving whispers ancient secrets. This cultural enthusiast's itinerary is meticulously crafted to provide a deep dive into the historical and artistic wonders that define Cambodia's heritage.

Day 1: Exploring the Marvels of Angkor Thom

Morning:

Begin your cultural immersion at Angkor Thom, the grand capital of the Khmer Empire. Start with the imposing South Gate and make your way to Bayon Temple, renowned for its 54 towers adorned with enigmatic faces. Marvel at the intricate bas-reliefs depicting historical events and daily life during the Khmer era.

Late Morning:

Visit the Terrace of the Elephants, a stunning platform adorned with carvings of elephants and other mythical creatures. Gain insights into the grandeur of Khmer architecture and its symbolic representations.

Afternoon:

Enjoy a traditional Khmer lunch at a local restaurant near Angkor

Thom. Savor authentic flavors and indulge in the local culinary scene.

Evening:

Embark on a serene exploration of Preah Khan, a temple complex that combines intricate carvings with a peaceful ambiance. Take your time to absorb the spiritual energy and historical significance.

Day 2: A Journey to Banteay Srei and Beyond

Early Morning:

Witness the sunrise at Banteay Srei, the "Citadel of Women." This pink sandstone temple boasts exquisite carvings and intricate details. Capture the morning light illuminating the delicate artwork.

Late Morning:

Explore the Angkor National Museum, a treasure trove of artifacts providing a comprehensive understanding of Khmer history and culture. Delve into the intricacies of Angkor's past before continuing your cultural journey.

Afternoon:

Venture to Banteay Samre, a lesser-known gem that mirrors the grandeur of Angkor Wat. Admire its well-preserved architecture and discover the symbolic significance of its carvings.

Evening:

Stroll through the enchanting Ta Prohm, famous for its fusion with nature. Explore the temple's labyrinthine passages adorned with tree roots, creating a captivating blend of man-made and natural artistry.

Day 3: Temple of Enlightenment – Angkor Wat

Morning:

Dedicate your morning to Angkor Wat, the crown jewel of Khmer architecture. Delve into the vast complex, exploring the central sanctuary, library, and galleries. Marvel at the intricate bas-reliefs depicting tales from Hindu mythology.

Late Morning:

Climb to the upper levels for panoramic views of the surrounding temples and jungles. Experience the spiritual aura that envelops Angkor Wat and reflect on the historical significance of this UNESCO World Heritage Site.

Afternoon:

Indulge in a leisurely lunch at a nearby restaurant, savoring the flavors of Khmer cuisine. Engage with locals to gain cultural insights and recommendations for hidden gems in the area.

Evening:

Cap off your cultural immersion at Phnom Bakheng, an ideal spot for a sunset spectacle. Witness the sun casting a warm glow over the temple complex, creating a magical atmosphere.

Accommodation Options:

1. Mid-Range Accommodation: Tara Angkor Hotel

Located in Siem Reap, this hotel provides pleasant rooms and easy access to Angkor Wat. Prices range from $60 to $120 per night.

2. Luxury Retreat: Belmond La Residence d'Angkor

This luxury resort combines traditional Khmer decor with modern comforts, providing an opulent experience. Prices start at $200 per night.

Dining recommendations:

1. Haven Restaurant:

A socially responsible restaurant that serves delicious Khmer and Western dishes. Enjoy a lunch while supporting a good cause.

2. Cuisine Wat Damnak:

Enjoy a fine dining experience with a changing menu including the best of Cambodian flavors.

Tips for Cultural Enthusiasts:

1. Connect with Locals:

Start interactions with locals to obtain a better grasp of Cambodian culture and traditions.

2. Respect the Temple Etiquette:

Follow the instructions for courteous behavior on temple grounds. Dress modestly and keep a peaceful posture.

3. Attend Cultural Performances:

Look for traditional Apsara dance performances in the evening for a fascinating peek into Khmer culture.

This cultural enthusiast's itinerary is designed to peel back the layers of Angkor Wat's cultural history, allowing you to soak up the essence of Cambodia's past while enjoying its colorful present.

3.3 Outdoor Adventure.

This outdoor adventure tour is tailored to individuals looking for an adrenaline rush amidst the historical wonders of Angkor Wat. Unleash your inner adventurer with hiking routes, zip-lining, and a variety of thrilling outdoor activities that fit in with the breathtaking scenery.

Day One: Conquering the Jungle Trails

Morning:

Take an early morning stroll through Angkor Thom's hidden jungle trails. Explore off-the-beaten-path roads, where you'll come across lesser-known temples and marvel at nature's ability to reclaim ancient ruins.

Late morning:

Hike to the top of Phnom Kulen, a sacred mountain treasured by the inhabitants. Discover the River of a Thousand Lingas, which is artistically etched into the riverbed, and take a refreshing swim in the Kulen Waterfall.

Afternoon:

Enjoy a picnic meal in the lovely surroundings. While navigating the jungle area, take some time to observe fauna.

Evening:

As the sun begins to set, return to Siem Reap for a well-earned dinner at a local restaurant. Relive your day's activities with Khmer specialties.

Day 2: Zip-line through the canopy

Morning:

Prepare for a fantastic day at the Angkor Zipline Eco-Adventure Park. Soar over the treetops while ziplining over the gorgeous Cambodian rainforest. Admire the panoramic views of the temples and surrounding countryside.

Late morning:

Continue the trip by seeing the Floating Village of Kompong Phluk. Explore the stilted cottages and learn about the locals' unusual lifestyle.

Afternoon:

Lunch in a floating restaurant, savoring fresh fish and local specialties. Take a kayaking or paddleboarding journey around the rivers that surround the village.

Evening:

Return to Siem Reap to unwind and relax after a busy day. A sunset ride on Tonle Sap Lake is a relaxing way to end your outdoor trip.

Day 3: Sunrise Hot Air Balloon Ride.

Early morning:

A sunrise hot air balloon flight over Angkor Wat is a one-of-a-kind experience. Soar far above the temples and see the sun cast its first light on the old monuments.

Late morning:

Descend from the skies and enjoy a substantial breakfast at a nearby café. Explore the Angkor Archaeological Park by mountain bike, navigating trails that provide a unique perspective of the temples.

Afternoon:

Visit Angkor Wat Zip-line Eco-Adventure Park for a unique zip-lining experience. Traverse the trees and experience the excitement of flying among historical wonders.

Evening:

Wrap up your outdoor excursion with a celebration dinner in Siem Reap. Choose from a variety of international and Khmer restaurants to round out your action-packed vacation.

Accommodation Options:

1. Angkor Palace Resort & Spa is a mid-range adventure hub.

Located near Angkor Wat, this resort provides comfortable accommodations with easy access to adventurous activities. Prices range from $80 to $150 per night.

2. Luxurious Jungle Retreat:

Nestled within beautiful nature, this magnificent retreat offers a peaceful environment after a day of outdoor activity. Prices start at $250 per night.

Dining recommendations:

1. Red Piano Restaurant:

A popular restaurant in Siem Reap with a broad menu and a lively environment. Perfect for post-adventure meals.

2. Marum:

A social enterprise restaurant offering delectable Khmer cuisine. While enjoying your culinary experience, you may contribute to a worthy cause.

Tips for Adventurers:

1. Pack accordingly:

For outdoor activities, dress comfortably, wick away perspiration, and wear sturdy shoes. Don't forget the sunscreen and insect repellent.

2. Stay hydrated:

Bring a reusable water bottle to remain hydrated on your outdoor outings. The Cambodian sun may be fierce.

3. Follow the Safety Guidelines:Follow the safety guidelines offered by adventure activity companies. Prioritize your health while enjoying the thrill.

This adventurer's schedule offers an adrenaline-fueled tour of Angkor Wat and its surroundings. From forest paths to zip-lining through the canopy, immerse yourself in the thrilling outdoor adventures that make Cambodia a one-of-a-kind and unforgettable destination for adventurers.

3.4 Family-Friendly Trip

A family-friendly vacation to Angkor Wat ensures a mix of historical exploration and enjoyable activities for all ages. This family-friendly schedule is carefully planned to deliver a great holiday filled with kid-friendly activities and fascinating experiences.

Day 1: Angkor Thom Adventures.

Morning:

Begin your family vacation with Angkor Thom, a huge complex that captivates visitors of all ages. Explore the Bayon Temple, which features the characteristic smiling faces that frequently attract children. The elaborate carvings and maze-like pathways create a lively environment for exploration.

Late morning:

Continue on to the Terrace of the Elephants, where children can admire the enormous platform covered with elephant carvings. Engage them in learning about the story behind the carvings and the historical significance of this monument.

Afternoon:

Lunch in a family-friendly restaurant near Angkor Thom. Choose traditional Khmer meals or worldwide favorites to meet everyone's tastes.

Evening:

Finish your day with a visit to Ta Prohm, a temple surrounded by massive tree roots. The magical atmosphere and adventurous surroundings make it an excellent choice for family adventure.

Day 2: Banteay Srei and Outside Activities

Morning:

Visit Banteay Srei, the "Citadel of Women," and admire the exquisite pink sandstone carvings that tell fascinating stories. Engage the kids in a scavenger quest to look for unusual carvings and symbols.

Late morning:

The Angkor National Museum features interactive exhibits that bring Khmer history to life. Children can enjoy educational games and activities that help them comprehend Cambodia's rich cultural history.

Afternoon:

Lunch at a family-friendly restaurant in Siem Reap, with a menu that includes selections for both adults and children. Consider eating local snacks and desserts to enhance the cultural flavor of your meal.

Evening:

Visit the Angkor Zipline Eco-Adventure Park for a day of family-friendly zip-lining. Soar through the treetops and see the excitement on your children's faces as they experience the rush of adventure.

Day 3: Angkor Wat Exploration and Family Relaxation.

Morning:

Begin your day with a tour to Angkor Wat, the pinnacle of Cambodian architecture. Engage the family in stories about ancient kingdoms and supernatural tales depicted in the temple's beautiful carvings.

Late morning:

Climb to the highest floors for panoramic vistas, allowing the kids to take in the enormity of the temple complex. Take family photos against the backdrop of this magnificent UNESCO World Heritage site.

Afternoon:

Enjoy a family-friendly meal at a restaurant near Angkor Wat. To accommodate a variety of tastes, use a blend of international and Khmer cuisine.

Evening:

Finish your family-friendly tour with a pleasant sunset boat ride on Tonle Sap Lake. Enjoy the calm of the lake while the youngsters spot local wildlife and traditional floating cottages.

Accommodation Options:

1. Sokha Angkor Resort is a family-friendly resort.

This resort, located near Angkor Wat, offers family suites and kid-friendly services. Prices range between $100 and $200 each night.

2. Homely Guesthouse: The Rose Apple Bed & Breakfast

A cozy guesthouse in Siem Reap that offers family-friendly accommodations. Prices start at $40 per night.

Dining recommendations:

1. Genevieve's Restaurant:

This family-friendly restaurant serves a variety of Western and Khmer meals. The inviting atmosphere makes it appropriate for youngsters.

2. Blue Pumpkins:

A popular destination for delectable pastries and ice cream. A delightful treat for the entire family after a day of sightseeing.

Tips for a Family-Friendly Vacation:

1. Stay hydrated:

Bring water bottles to stay hydrated, especially in the Cambodian heat. Ensure that everyone takes regular breaks to rest and drink water.

2. Educational games:

Use educational activities or a travel journal to keep children interested during historical trips. Encourage them to record their impressions and favorite moments.

3. Flexible itinerary:

Keep a flexible timetable that allows for spontaneous pauses or further exploration based on the family's interests.

This family-friendly schedule ensures a healthy balance of cultural exploration and entertainment activities, resulting in memorable memories for all members of the family. From ancient temples to outdoor excursions, Angkor Wat has something for everyone, making it an excellent choice for a memorable family vacation.

3.5 Budget Travel

Going on a low-budget trip to Angkor Wat does not mean sacrificing the awe-inspiring experience of discovering ancient monuments and rich history. This cost-effective schedule is designed for budget-conscious tourists, offering a stimulating experience without breaking the bank.

Day 1: Siem Reap Exploration.

Morning:

Arrive in Siem Reap and settle into a low-cost hotel like Green Valley Guesthouse, where rates start at $20 a night. Begin the day with a healthy breakfast at a local restaurant, where meals like Khmer noodles or rice and vegetable stir-fry can be had for as little as $2-4.

Late morning:

Embark on a self-guided walking tour of Siem Reap, visiting the Old Market and Pub Street. Engage with local sellers and look for inexpensive items. Admission to these locations is free, so you may fully immerse yourself in the dynamic ambiance without spending any money.

Afternoon:

Have a simple and delicious meal at a local market or street food seller. Prices for meals can range from $2 to $5. Consider having a cup of traditional Khmer soup or a refreshing fruit smoothie.

Evening:

Choose a budget-friendly supper at a neighborhood restaurant. Street food selections are not only inexpensive, but also offer a sense of true Cambodian cuisine. Finish your day with a trip to the Night Market, where you can explore inexpensive handicrafts and fabrics.

Day Two: Temple Exploration

Morning:

Start your day early by visiting Angkor Wat for sunrise. Buy a one-day Angkor Pass for $37. Save money on food by packing a simple breakfast from a nearby bakery or market.

Late morning:

Explore Angkor Wat's stunning architecture and beautiful carvings. Take advantage of free guided tours provided by students near the temple entrance. These excursions provide useful information about the history and significance of Angkor Wat.

Afternoon:

Lunch at a local restaurant in Siem Reap or near the temples, where you can find affordable selections ranging from $3 to $8. Consider attempting a classic Khmer curry or a vegetable-based rice meal.

Evening:

Finish your temple tour with a visit to Phnom Bakheng for a panoramic sunset vista. Entry to Phnom Bakheng is included in your Angkor Pass. Return to Siem Reap for a reasonably priced meal at one of the local markets or street food vendors.

Day 3: Outdoor Adventure for a Budget

Morning:

Take a cheap trip to Kulen Waterfall, which is roughly 50 kilometers from Siem Reap. Hire a tuk-tuk for a day trip, which often costs $30-40. Admission to Kulen Waterfall costs about $20, including transportation.

Late morning:

Explore the stunning waterfall and have a picnic lunch at the location. You can bring your own food and drinks to keep costs down.

Afternoon:

On your return trip to Siem Reap, stop by the River of a Thousand Lingas and Banteay Srei. Your Angkor Pass covers the entrance prices to these sites. Return to Siem Reap for a reasonably priced meal at a local restaurant.

Evening:

Finish off your budget-friendly tour with a peaceful evening at Pub Street. Enjoy the lively atmosphere and maybe try a local beer or some delicious coconut water.

Accommodation Options:

1. Cost-effective Guesthouse: Rosy Guesthouse

Located in Siem Reap, this guesthouse provides cheap rooms from at $15 per night.

2. Hotel Accommodation: Onederz Cambodia

A budget-friendly hostel with dormitory beds starting at $8 a night.

Dining recommendations:

1. The Khmer Kitchen Restaurant:

A neighborhood café that serves affordable Khmer cuisine. Prices range from $3 to $8 each lunch.

2. Street Food Stalls Near Pub Street

Try a variety of street food alternatives for cheap and tasty local fare.

Tips for Budget-Conscious Travelers

1. Local Transport:

Explore Siem Reap and the temples on a budget by taking tuk-tuks or bicycles.

2. Free activities: Take advantage of free activities include as walking tours, browsing local markets, and experiencing Siem Reap's dynamic atmosphere.

3. Pack Snacks:

- Bring food and drinks from local stores to keep costs down for your temple visits and outdoor excursions.

This budget-friendly schedule ensures that budget-conscious guests can enjoy the glories of Angkor Wat without sacrificing the richness of the journey. This plan provides a rewarding journey on a restricted budget, from low-cost lodging to seeing local markets and eating at budget-friendly restaurants.

Chapter 4: Accommodation

4.1 Overview of Accommodation Options.

Choosing the proper lodging is an important part of arranging your trip to Angkor Wat. The region provides a varied choice of accommodations to suit a variety of preferences and budgets. Understanding the many types of accommodations available ensures a relaxing and happy stay in this interesting destination.

Hotels

Location:

Siem Reap, the gateway to Angkor Wat, has a wide choice of hotels, from affordable to luxury, spread across the city. You'll discover options near the Angkor Archaeological Park, which provide easy access to the temples.

Cost:

Budget Hotels: With rates as low as $20 a night, budget hotels provide clean and basic amenities for guests on a tight budget.

Mid-Range Hotels: Priced between $50 and $100 per night, mid-range hotels offer more comfort and amenities.

Luxury Hotels: High-end luxury hotels, which cost more than $150 a night, provide sumptuous experiences with lavish accommodations and premium services.

Highlights:

Luxury options, such as Belmond La Résidence d'Angkor, provide a tranquil respite, and mid-range options, such as Tara Angkor Hotel, strike a compromise between comfort and price. Budget-friendly solutions, such as Green Valley Guesthouse, cater to individuals who want simplicity.

Resorts.

Location:

Siem Reap is mostly home to luxury resorts, many of which include spa facilities and spacious gardens. Some resorts have private access to Angkor Wat, creating an exclusive and serene atmosphere.

Cost:

Luxury Resorts: High-end resorts can cost between $200 and $500 per night and provide quality amenities, personalized services, and a relaxing ambiance.

Highlights:

Consider the luxury Phum Baitang Resort or the serene Sokha Angkor Resort. These resorts frequently offer one-of-a-kind architectural features and beautiful surroundings, making them ideal for unwinding after a day of adventure.

Guesthouses

Location:

Guesthouses are dotted throughout Siem Reap and provide a more intimate and local experience. Some may be located closer to the city center, with convenient access to dining and shopping.

Cost:

Guesthouses: Prices vary but are typically lower than hotels, ranging from $15 to $50 per night. This option is ideal for people who want a more personalized and local touch.

Highlights:

The Rose Apple Bed & Breakfast is a beautiful guesthouse that offers a comfortable atmosphere. Guesthouses frequently provide insights into local culture and might be an excellent option for budget-conscious travelers.

Hostels

Location:

Hostels that cater to budget travelers and backpackers are mainly located in Siem Reap's core regions. They offer shared lodgings and common areas.

Cost:

Hostels: Prices are the most affordable, starting at $8 per night for dormitory beds. Private rooms in hostels may be provided for a slightly additional cost.

Highlights:

Onederz Cambodia is a renowned hostel that provides cheap without sacrificing cleanliness and comfort. Hostels are perfect for single travelers or those who want to meet like-minded people.

Unique Stays

Location:

Siem Reap offers a variety of distinctive accommodations, including traditional Khmer-style lodgings and eco-friendly options. These accommodations provide a different and engaging experience.

Cost:*

Unique Stays: Prices vary depending on the type of accommodation. Traditional Khmer homestays or eco-friendly hotels may cost $30 to $100 per night.

Highlights:

Consider Phare, The Cambodian Circus Homestay for an unforgettable cultural experience. Unique stays allow you to engage with local communities and promote sustainable tourist practices.

Selecting the Right Accommodation for You

1. Budget considerations:

Determine your budget and research possibilities inside that range. Siem Reap has accommodation for all budgets, so there's something for everyone.

2. Proximity to Angkor Wat

If viewing the temples is a top priority, consider lodging near the Angkor Archaeological Park for convenient access to Angkor Wat and other major attractions.

3. Amenities and services:

Consider the amenities available, such as Wi-Fi, breakfast, and transportation services. Spas and private trips are examples of luxury alternatives.

4. Local experience:

For a more immersive local experience, stay in guesthouses or other unusual lodgings. This enables you to engage with the community and get cultural insights.

5. Review and Recommendation:

Read reviews from other travelers to get a sense of what they experienced. Websites such as TripAdvisor and Booking.com provide useful information about the quality of accommodations.

Booking Tips and Tricks

1. Book In Advance:

Booking in early, particularly during peak seasons, ensures availability and may result in discounts.

2. Look for Packages:

Some accommodations have bundled packages that include tours, food, and transportation, which adds value.

3. Consider Local Homestays:

For a genuinely authentic experience, look into local homestays, where you can interact with people and learn about their way of life.

4. Check Cancellation Policies:

Before confirming your reservation, read the cancellation

regulations to avoid any inconveniences.

To summarize, Siem Reap offers a varied range of hotel options to meet any traveler's preferences and budget. Whether you choose luxury, a local experience, or a low-cost lodging, knowing your alternatives can help you have a comfortable and pleasurable stay while exploring Angkor Wat.

4.2 Luxury Resorts

For anyone looking for a unique and opulent experience while visiting the glories of Angkor Wat, the region has a number of top-tier luxury resorts. These institutions not only offer lavish lodgings, but they also immerse tourists in Cambodia's rich cultural and natural heritage.

1. Phum Baitang Resort

Location:

Phum Baitang Resort, located just minutes from Angkor Wat, is a quiet retreat surrounded by green rice terraces and palm trees. Its quiet location provides a peaceful retreat while keeping close to the archaeological wonders.

Accommodations:

The resort has 45 traditional wooden villas, each beautifully equipped with a mix of rustic charm and modern luxury. Guests can select between Terrace Villas with private plunge pools and large Pool Villas for maximum solitude.

Amenities:

Phum Baitang provides a variety of amenities, including a spa with rejuvenating treatments, two restaurants providing excellent Khmer and foreign cuisine, and a stunning infinity pool surrounded by lush vegetation.

Cultural touch:

The resort is built to resemble a rural Cambodian village, offering tourists an authentic cultural experience. The resort's on-site organic farm adds to its commitment to sustainability and community involvement.

Cost:

Indulging in the opulence of Phum Baitang costs $250 per night, making it an exclusive option for those wanting a sumptuous hideaway.

2. Belmond La Résidence D'Angkor

Location:

Belmond La Résidence d'Angkor, located along the Siem Reap River, is well situated for quick access to Angkor Wat and Siem Reap's lively marketplaces.

Accommodations:

This luxurious hideaway has 59 suites decorated with traditional Cambodian artwork and modern conveniences. The large Deluxe Suites include private terraces, and the Pool Suites have direct access to a verdant courtyard.

Amenities:

Guests can relax in the hotel's enormous saltwater pool, unwind in the Kong Kea Spa, and eat delicious meals at the on-site restaurants. The Elephant Bar is ideal for sipping a cocktail and reminiscing on your day's travels.

Cultural touch:

Belmond La Résidence d'Angkor hosts traditional Apsara dance performances, giving guests a taste of Cambodia's rich cultural history.

Cost:

Indulge in the elegant ambiance of Belmond La Résidence d'Angkor, which starts at $200 per night and offers a magnificent refuge in Siem Reap.

3. Amansara

Location:

Amansara, formerly King Norodom Sihanouk's guest villa, is located in the middle of Siem Reap and features a historical setting surrounded by gardens.

Accommodations:

With only 24 suites, Amansara provides an intimate and personal experience. The suites combine modern minimalism with traditional Khmer style, providing a polished and elegant ambiance.

Amenities:

The resort includes a spa, a beautiful swimming pool, and several eating options. Guests can explore the Angkor temples using personalized itineraries designed by the resort's skilled guides.

Cultural touch:

Amansara's historical significance gives a distinct cultural touch, educating tourists about Cambodia's royal heritage. The resort provides tailored experiences, such as excursions to nearby towns and special temple tours.

Cost:

Experiencing the luxury of Amansara starts at $800 a night, catering to those seeking the pinnacle of exclusivity and customized service.

4. Raffles Grand Hotel d'Angkor

Location:

Raffles Grand Hotel d'Angkor, located near the heart of Siem Reap, exudes colonial elegance and timeless luxury.

Accommodations:

This iconic hotel has a variety of exquisite rooms, such as State Rooms, Landmark Rooms, and the ultra-luxurious Personality Suites. Each room is precisely created, combining antique and contemporary aspects.

Amenities:

Guests can relax in the lovely gardens, swim in the pool, or dine at the hotel's acclaimed restaurants. The Apsara Terrace showcases traditional dance performances in a lovely outdoor setting.

Cultural touch:

Raffles Grand Hotel d'Angkor, with its historical appeal, transports guests back in time. The hotel's architecture and decor evoke the grandeur of the colonial past.

Cost:

Embracing the grandeur of Raffles Grand Hotel d'Angkor begins at $250 per night and provides an elegant hideaway with a touch of Cambodian history.

Finally, these luxury resorts serve as portals to Angkor Wat's cultural and historical treasures, in addition to providing magnificent accommodations. While the prices reflect the exclusivity of these activities, they offer an amazing voyage that combines pleasure with Cambodia's rich legacy.

4.3 Budget-Friendly Hotels

When visiting the stunning wonders of Angkor Wat on a budget, discerning tourists will find a variety of pleasant and reasonable accommodations in Siem Reap. These low-cost hotels strike the ideal balance between affordability and convenience, offering a comfortable stay while preserving the essence of the Cambodian experience.

1. Green Valley Guesthouse

Location:

Green Valley Guesthouse, located in the middle of Siem Reap, offers convenient access to both the city's dynamic atmosphere and the surrounding Angkor Archaeological Park.

Accommodations:

This guesthouse offers clean, basic accommodations, making it an excellent alternative for budget-conscious guests. The rooms are outfitted with essential conveniences to guarantee a comfortable stay.

Amenities:

While Green Valley Guesthouse may not have expensive amenities, it does give important services such as free Wi-Fi, a shared sitting space, and tour help.

Cost:

Green Valley Guesthouse offers to guests looking for affordability without sacrificing convenience, with rates starting at $20 a night.

2. Rosy Guesthouse

Location:

Rosy Guesthouse is conveniently located near Siem Reap's Old Market district, providing easy access to a variety of dining options, retail malls, and the popular Pub Street.

Accommodations:

Rosy Guesthouse offers a variety of affordable rooms, including dormitory-style accommodations for lone travelers and those on a limited budget. Private rooms and shared facilities are also available.

Amenities:

Guests can take advantage of complimentary Wi-Fi, a shared kitchen, and a comfortable common room. The guesthouse provides travel services, assisting guests in planning their trips around Angkor Wat.

Cost:

Rosy Guesthouse, with rates starting at $15 per night, is an affordable option for tourists looking for a friendly and social environment.

3. Onederz Cambodia.

Location:

Onederz Cambodia is centrally placed in Siem Reap, making it an ideal location for seeing both the city's attractions and the adjacent temples.

Accommodations:

This hostel provides a range of dormitory bedrooms and shared facilities. The dormitories include privacy partitions for enhanced comfort. Private rooms are also available for those who like a bit more privacy.

Amenities:

Onederz Cambodia offers complimentary Wi-Fi, a common lounge, and a rooftop terrace from which guests may mingle and enjoy panoramic views. The hostel provides a variety of activities to build a vibrant and community environment.

Cost:

With dormitory beds starting at $8 a night, Onederz Cambodia is an excellent choice for budget-conscious travelers seeking a friendly and lively setting.

4. The Rose Apple Bed and Breakfast

Location:

The Rose Apple Bed & Breakfast, located in a quiet neighborhood, provides a peaceful respite while keeping within a fair distance of Siem Reap's bustling attractions.

Accommodations:

This quaint guesthouse features pleasant rooms with Khmer-inspired decor. The accommodations are intended to provide a welcoming environment for guests.

Amenities:

The Rose Apple Bed & Breakfast has free Wi-Fi, a garden for relaxation, and personalized services. Guests can enjoy authentic Khmer hospitality during their stay.

Cost:

The Rose Apple Bed & Breakfast offers pricing starting at $40 per night, striking a mix between affordability and a more customized guest experience.

In summary, these budget-friendly hotels in Siem Reap meet the practical needs of guests looking for low-cost accommodations without sacrificing comfort. From guesthouses to hostels, these options offer a variety of possibilities for anyone looking to explore the grandeur of Angkor Wat on a budget.

4.4 Boutique Guesthouses

Boutique guesthouses in Siem Reap provide a delightful alternative to popular hotels for guests looking for an intimate and one-of-a-kind experience while visiting Angkor Wat. These establishments, which are generally distinguished by their unique design, customized service, and cultural milieu, offer a lovely escape for people who want a more private atmosphere.

1. Viroth's Hotel

Location:

Viroth's Hotel, nestled in a quiet neighborhood near the heart of Siem Reap, is a boutique jewel. It offers a peaceful escape while still providing convenient access to the city's main attractions.

Accommodations:

The hotel's rooms are tastefully arranged, featuring contemporary Khmer art and locally crafted furnishings. Each room exemplifies a perfect blend of modern comfort and traditional design.

Amenities:

Viroth's Hotel features an appealing swimming pool surrounded by beautiful foliage, a spa for relaxation, and a restaurant that serves a combination of Khmer and foreign cuisine. The helpful personnel personalized the client experience.

Cultural touch:

The architecture and décor pay homage to Cambodia's rich cultural past, delivering a fully immersive experience for tourists.

Cost:

Viroth's Hotel's boutique luxury begins from $150 a night and provides a one-of-a-kind and culturally rich retreat.

2. Jaya House River Park

Location:

Jaya House RiverPark, located along the Siem Reap River, offers a serene location while remaining conveniently near to the city's lively markets and attractions.

Accommodations:

The boutique guesthouse has spacious and attractively decorated rooms, with an emphasis on sustainability. Guests can pick between accommodations with private balconies that overlook the river and those with direct access to the lovely gardens.

Amenities:

Jaya House RiverPark is committed to environmentally friendly operations, including a zero-waste restaurant, a beautiful saltwater pool, and spa facilities. The guesthouse also provides bicycles for guests to explore the area.

Cultural touch:

The guesthouse actively participates in the local community and supports a variety of social and environmental programs, giving guests the opportunity to contribute to responsible tourism.

Cost:

The eco-luxury of Jaya House RiverPark starts about $200 per night and promises a sustainable and culturally enriching stay.

3. Baby Elephant Boutique Hotel

Location:

Baby Elephant Boutique Hotel is conveniently placed in Siem Reap, near the city center and the archaeological wonders of Angkor Wat.

Accommodations:

This boutique hotel's rooms are meticulously furnished, with an emphasis on comfort and elegance. Guests can select between huge suites and intimate rooms, each with its own unique decor.

Amenities:

The hotel features a refreshing pool, a rooftop bar with panoramic views, and a restaurant serving Khmer and international cuisine. Yoga sessions and wellness activities enhance the overall guest experience.

Cultural touch:

Baby Elephant Boutique Hotel actively supports local artists and artisans by displaying their work throughout the facility. The hotel also contributes to neighborhood initiatives, creating a significant cultural connection.

Cost:

Experiencing the charm of Baby Elephant Boutique Hotel begins about $80 per night, providing an economical yet carefully tailored stay.

4. Maison Polonka

Location:

Maison Polanka, located in a calm area of Siem Reap, offers a hidden refuge while remaining close to the city's attractions.

Accommodations:

This boutique guesthouse features a variety of private villas and suites, each with its own distinct character and decor. Guests can enjoy the seclusion of their own room, surrounded by gorgeous tropical vegetation.

Amenities:

Maison Polanka has a refreshing pool, a spa for relaxation, and a restaurant providing gourmet food. The attentive team provides a personalized and immersive experience.

Cultural touch:

The guesthouse's architecture resembles traditional Khmer design, and the attentive staff shares information about local customs and traditions.

Cost:

The calm luxury of Maison Polanka starts at around $250 per night and provides a unique and culturally immersive getaway.

To summarize, boutique guesthouses in Siem Reap offer an intriguing alternative for guests wanting a more customized and culturally rich experience. From eco-friendly practices to innovative designs, these hotels provide a lovely respite while visiting the grandeur of Angkor Wat.

4.5 Unique Stays

For guests seeking an unusual and unorthodox experience in Angkor Wat, Siem Reap offers a variety of one-of-a-kind lodging options that go beyond regular hotels. These unusual lodgings provide an opportunity to immerse oneself in the local culture, architecture, and natural surroundings, resulting in an amazing and unique journey.

1. Phare: The Cambodian Circus Homestay

Location:

The Cambodian Circus Homestay, located on the busy Pub Street in Phare, provides a unique blend of cultural immersion and entertainment.

Accommodations:

The homestay has pleasant rooms decorated with vivid artwork created by artists from the Phare Ponleu Selpak Circus. Each room offers a pleasant and artistic refuge.

Amenities:

Guests can watch nightly circus shows in the adjacent Big Top, where artists exhibit their skills. The guesthouse actively supports the Phare Ponleu Selpak NGO, which promotes community development.

Cultural touch:

The entire experience at Phare, The Cambodian Circus Homestay is focused on supporting local artists and participating with the community.

Cost:

The Cambodian Circus Homestay, set amid the artistic ambiance of Phare, starts at around $30 per night and provides a budget-friendly and culturally rich stay.

2. Templation by MAADS

Location:

Set against a backdrop of lush foliage and quiet scenery, Templation by MAADS offers a tranquil getaway close to Angkor Wat.

Accommodations:

This one-of-a-kind stay features a mix of minimalist villas and suites, each with private plunge pools and a modern aesthetic. The lodgings fit in perfectly with the natural surroundings.

Amenities:

Templation by MAADS has a huge saltwater pool, a spa with revitalizing treatments, and an on-site restaurant serving Khmer and foreign cuisine.

Natural Touch:

The resort's architecture blends with nature, adopting sustainable principles while giving a calm getaway from the hustle and bustle of daily life.

Cost:

Indulge in the quiet luxury of Templation by MAADS, which starts at around $200 per night and provides an environmentally responsible and tranquil experience.

3. Floating Village Homestay

Location:

The Floating town Homestay offers a totally authentic experience by allowing guests to stay in a traditional stilted house within the Kampong Phluk floating town.

Accommodations:

The homestay provides simple but authentic accommodations, allowing guests to experience daily life in the floating village. Stilted dwellings offer a unique look at Cambodian village life.

Amenities:

Guests can explore the floating hamlet by boat, see local customs, and take part in community events. The homestay provides a genuine glimpse into the hardships and joys of living on the sea.

Cultural touch:

The Floating Village Homestay offers an unprecedented opportunity to interact with the local inhabitants and obtain a better knowledge of their way of life.

Cost:

Immersing oneself in the floating village experience costs around $50 per night and provides an off-the-beaten-path excursion.

4. Four Rivers Floating Lodge

Location:

Nestled on the verdant Tatai River, 4 Rivers Floating Lodge

provides a peaceful retreat surrounded by nature.

Accommodations:

The lodge's floating tented villas blend luxury with an immersive nature environment. Each villa offers a private balcony with spectacular views of the river and forests.

Amenities:

Guests can explore the nearby wilderness by kayaking, jungle walking, or taking a boat tour. The on-site restaurant serves a broad cuisine that highlights local flavors.

Natural Touch:

4 Rivers Floating Lodge offers an eco-friendly vacation that uses solar power and sustainable measures to reduce its environmental impact.

Cost:

An eco-luxury retreat at 4 Rivers Floating Lodge starts from $250 per night and provides a unique blend of comfort and nature.

Finally, these one-of-a-kind lodgings in Siem Reap are ideal for daring tourists looking for a unique experience. These unique accommodations, ranging from cultural immersion to natural retreats, promise an unforgettable adventure beyond the usual.

4.6 Most Recommended Hotels and Resorts

Editor's Picks for an unforgettable stay

When planning a trip to Angkor Wat, the type of lodging you choose can have a significant impact on your overall experience. To help you choose the ideal accommodation, we've compiled a selection of top-rated hotels and resorts in Siem Reap that offer an amazing and immersive stay.

1. Shinta Manicure Shack

Location:

Shinta Mani Shack, centrally located in the French Quarter,

combines modern elegance with Khmer-inspired décor. Its proximity to Pub Street and the Angkor Archaeological Park makes it an ideal alternative.

Accommodations:

The hotel offers nicely designed rooms and suites with modern conveniences. The Shinta Mani Spa offers a variety of rejuvenating treatments, while the hotel's Kroya Restaurant gives a lovely dining experience.

Cost:

Shinta Mani Shack offers exquisite elegance starting at $150 per night.

2. Anantara Angkor Resort

Location:

Anantara Angkor Resort, located near the Angkor Wat temple

complex, offers a relaxing retreat with convenient access to the famed archeological monuments.

Accommodations:

The resort has huge suites and pool villas, each with a mix of traditional Khmer architecture and modern amenities. Guests can unwind at the spa or enjoy fine dining at Chi Restaurant.

Cost:

Experiencing the peacefulness of Anantara Angkor Resort starts from $200 per night.

3. Park Hyatt Siem Reap

Location:

Park Hyatt Siem Reap is a magnificent hideaway located in the city center, just a short walk from the Old Market and Pub Street.

Accommodations:

The hotel offers exquisite rooms and suites with Khmer-inspired décor. Guests can relax at the spa, swim in the pool, and eat gourmet meals at The Dining Room.

Cost:

Embracing the luxury of Park Hyatt Siem Reap starts from $250 per night.

4. Rambutan Resort - Siem Reap

Location:

Rambutan Resort, conveniently located near the city center, offers a calm refuge with easy access to the city's lively markets and nightlife.

Accommodations:

The resort features a variety of beautiful rooms and suites surrounded by lovely grounds. Guests can relax by the pool, get spa treatments, and eat at the on-site restaurant.

Cost:

The laid-back luxury of Rambutan Resort starts around $80 per night.

5. FCC Angkor, managed by Avani.

Location:

FCC Angkor, maintained by Avani, is tucked beside the Siem Reap River, providing a peaceful environment near the city's attractions.

Accommodations:

The hotel's rooms and suites are well-appointed, featuring a mix of modern amenities and Colonial elegance. Guests can relax by the pool, visit the spa, and eat delicious meals at the Mansion Restaurant.

Cost:

Indulge in the riverside luxury of FCC Angkor, which starts around $120 per night.

4.7 Selecting the Right Accommodation for You

Factors to Consider When Booking Your Stay

Choosing the appropriate lodging is essential for a memorable visit in Angkor Wat. Consider the following considerations to guarantee your chosen stay meets your needs and improves your entire experience:

1. Location Proximity

Choose accommodations that are appropriate for your travel itinerary. If you intend to see the temples extensively, choose a hotel near Angkor Wat. For individuals who enjoy the city's nightlife, a central position near Pub Street may be excellent.

2. Budget

Set a budget for your stay and look at options that are within your price range. Siem Reap has a wide selection of lodgings, from low-cost guesthouses to luxury resorts.

3. Amenities and Facilities

Consider the amenities provided by the accommodation. If you want to unwind, seek for a property with a spa or pool. For people who like culinary experiences, choose a hotel with a variety of eating alternatives.

4. Cultural Immersion

If cultural immersion is critical, select accommodations that reflect local customs and aesthetics. Boutique hotels and guesthouses typically offer a more authentic experience.

5. Reviews & Ratings

Read reviews from other travelers to learn about previous visitors' experiences. Websites such as TripAdvisor and Booking.com provide useful reviews to help you make an informed decision.

6. Sustainable Practices

Consider environmentally friendly accomodation. Some hotels in

Siem Reap are dedicated to environmental sustainability and community involvement.

4.8 Booking Tips and Tricks

Strategies for Getting the Best Accommodation Deals

Securing the greatest lodging deals necessitates a planned strategy. Follow these suggestions and strategies to maximize your budget and have a good stay at Angkor Wat:

1. Book In Advance:

Secure your lodging early to get better rates and ensure availability, especially during peak travel seasons.

2. Flexible dates:

If you have flexible travel dates, consider internet platforms that allow you to compare fares across many days. Adjusting your stay by a day or two can result in big savings.

3. Travel packages:

Consider travel packages that include accommodations, flights, and activities. Some packages include discounts for bundling services.

4. Loyalty Programs:

Join hotel businesses' loyalty programs to receive potential discounts, room upgrades, and other benefits. Collect points for future stays.

5. Off-Peak Travel:

Consider traveling during off-peak seasons, when lodging prices are typically lower. You'll also have a more tranquil experience at popular attractions.

6. Price Comparison Websites:

Use online tools to compare prices from multiple booking sites. This ensures that you receive the most competitive pricing for your chosen stay.

7. Look For Promotions:

Check the hotel's website for specials, discounts, and special offers. Some specials are limited to the hotel's own booking platform.

8. Contact the hotel directly.

After discovering a good deal online, call the hotel directly to see if they can provide a better value or additional benefits.

9. Consider Refundable Rates:

While non-refundable prices may be less expensive, consider refundable rates, especially if your plans are flexible. This flexibility can be beneficial.

Consider these aspects and use smart booking tactics to acquire the best accommodation for your interests and budget, ensuring a memorable and pleasant stay in Angkor Wat.

Chapter 5: Iconic Places and Attractions

5.1 Angkor Wat Temple

In-depth Exploration of the Main Temple

Angkor Wat, a UNESCO World Heritage site, stands as one of the most magnificent and iconic temples in the world. As the largest religious monument globally, this ancient marvel beckons travelers to delve into its rich history and intricate architecture.

History:

Built in the 12th century by King Suryavarman II, Angkor Wat was initially dedicated to the Hindu god Vishnu and later transformed into a Buddhist temple. The sprawling complex reflects the Khmer Empire's grandeur and artistic achievements during its peak.

Architectural Marvels:

Angkor Wat is renowned for its stunning Khmer architecture, characterized by intricate bas-reliefs, towering spires, and vast courtyards. The central tower represents Mount Meru, the abode of the gods in Hindu mythology, symbolizing the connection between the earthly and divine realms.

Exploration Tips:

Begin your exploration early in the morning to witness the mesmerizing sunrise over Angkor Wat. The changing colors of the sky provide a captivating backdrop to the temple's silhouette.

Navigate the temple's corridors and galleries to discover detailed bas-reliefs depicting scenes from Hindu epics and ancient Khmer life. The east and west bas-reliefs tell distinct stories, offering a visual narrative of the Khmer civilization.

Sunrise and Sunset Viewing Tips

Sunrise:

Arrive at the temple complex before dawn to secure a prime spot for sunrise viewing. The iconic reflection of Angkor Wat in the lotus pond adds to the ethereal experience.

Consider hiring a local guide who can guide you to the best vantage points and share insights into the temple's history and significance.

Sunset:

Explore the western side of Angkor Wat for sunset views, capturing the temple against the changing hues of the evening sky.

Climb to elevated spots, such as Phnom Bakheng or Pre Rup, to witness panoramic sunset vistas over the entire Angkor archaeological park.

5.2 Bayon Temple

Discovering the Mystical Smiling Faces

Nestled at the heart of Angkor Thom, the Bayon Temple is renowned for its enigmatic smiling faces, creating an aura of mystique and spiritual reverence.

Architectural Marvels:

Built by King Jayavarman VII in the late 12th century, Bayon is a unique blend of Mahayana Buddhist and traditional Khmer architectural styles. The temple is adorned with 54 towers, each featuring four faces believed to represent the bodhisattva Avalokiteshvara or the king himself.

Mystical Smiling Faces:

The Bayon's most iconic feature is the multitude of stone faces adorning the towers. These serene and enigmatic smiles, looking out in all directions, evoke a sense of calm and contemplation. The intricate detailing of the faces adds to the temple's allure.

Recommended Times for Visit:

Morning Hours: Visit Bayon early in the morning to experience a tranquil atmosphere before the crowds arrive. The soft morning light enhances the temple's mystique.

Late Afternoon: As the day wanes, explore Bayon during the late afternoon to witness the changing play of light on the stone faces, creating captivating shadows and highlights.

Exploration Tips:

Traverse Bayon's labyrinthine corridors and ascend its narrow staircases to reach different levels, offering varying perspectives of the temple complex.

Engage with local guides to unravel the symbolic meanings behind the intricate carvings and bas-reliefs, providing insights into the historical and religious significance of Bayon.

5.3 Ta Prohm Temple

Exploring the Jungle Temple

Tucked away in the sprawling Angkor Archaeological Park, Ta Prohm Temple stands as a captivating testament to the intertwining forces of nature and ancient architecture. Famously known as the "Jungle Temple," Ta Prohm enchants visitors with its mystical atmosphere, where ancient stone structures coexist harmoniously with the surrounding jungle.

Historical Background:

Built in the late 12th and early 13th centuries by King Jayavarman VII, Ta Prohm served as a Buddhist monastery and university. The temple complex was dedicated to the king's mother and features a series of interconnected enclosures, courtyards, and intricate stone structures.

Architectural Marvels:

Ta Prohm's allure lies in its unique state of preservation – or rather, partial overgrowth. Unlike many other temples in the Angkor complex, Ta Prohm has been intentionally left in a semi-ruined state, allowing the encroaching jungle to weave its way through the stone structures.

Unique Features:

Giant Spung Trees: Towering spung trees with extensive root systems envelop parts of the temple, creating a surreal and captivating sight. The roots intertwine with the stone walls, creating an intricate mesh that seems both natural and man-made.

Hall of Dancers: The eastern section of Ta Prohm features the Hall of Dancers, adorned with exquisite carvings depicting celestial dancers. The intricate bas-reliefs provide a glimpse into the artistic and cultural richness of the Khmer Empire.

Photography Tips

Capturing the essence of Ta Prohm necessitates a sharp eye for detail and knowledge of the temple's distinguishing traits. Here are some photography suggestions to make the most of your visit:

1. Golden Hours: Visit Ta Prohm in the early morning or late afternoon to photograph the temple in soft, golden light. This not only warms up your images, but also highlights the contrast between the stone structures and the surrounding flora.

2. Silhouettes and Shadows: Take advantage of the interplay of light and shadow created by the forest canopy. Use the filtered sunlight to create eye-catching silhouettes against the temple walls, highlighting the delicate intricacies.

3. Wide-angle Shots: Due to Ta Prohm's extensive and intricate root systems, wide-angle lenses are great for capturing the temple's grandeur and highlighting the delicate intricacies of the stone sculptures against the jungle backdrop.

4. Close-up Details: Examine Ta Prohm's distinctive features, including elaborate carvings, moss-covered stones, and interwoven tree roots. These close-up photos offer a more detailed understanding of the temple's texture and history.

5. Capture the Contrast: Showcase the coexistence of nature and old building by taking photos that demonstrate the contrast between moss-covered stones, vivid vegetation, and worn temple structures.

6. People and immensity: Incorporate human components into your photographs to illustrate the immensity of Ta Prohm. Human presence, whether it's other people exploring the temple or local guides providing information, adds a dynamic touch to your photos.

Conservation efforts

Ta Prohm's delicate blend of environment and heritage presents unique conservation problems. Efforts are underway to protect the temple's structural integrity while retaining its characteristic overgrown appearance. Conservation workers work methodically to stabilize walls, restore carvings, and assure visitors' safety.

Accessibility and Visitor Tips.

Location: Ta Prohm is located around 1.5 kilometers east of Angkor Thom and Bayon Temple. It's conveniently accessible within the Angkor Archaeological Park.

Entry Requirements: A valid Angkor Pass is necessary to enter Ta Prohm. Passes can be purchased at the park's main gate.

Guided Tours: Consider hiring a local guide to help you better grasp Ta Prohm's history and significance. Guides can explain the temple's distinctive features and tell stories about its discovery.

Appropriate Attire: As with other temples in the Angkor complex, visitors are urged to dress modestly, with shoulders and knees covered as a show of respect.

Early Visit: Ta Prohm is less busy in the early morning, allowing for a more quiet and immersive experience. Early visits also provide great lighting for photography.

To summarize, a visit to Ta Prohm Temple is a trip into the mystical embrace of nature and history. Ta Prohm, with its convoluted tunnels and delicate dance between stone and root, exposes a unique chapter in the story of Angkor's ancient wonders.

Capture the essence of this jungle temple through creative photography, learn about its history, and admire the careful attempts to preserve its timeless beauty.

5.4 Angkor Thom

The Grand City and Its Marvels

Nestled in the center of the Angkor Archaeological Park, Angkor Thom exemplifies the Khmer Empire's magnificence and architectural prowess. Angkor Thom, which translates as "Great City," was the Khmer Empire's last and most durable capital during the reign of King Jayavarman VII. The sprawling complex, ringed by a massive moat, includes a multiplicity of temples, royal mansions, and spectacular monuments.

South Gate:

The South Gate, a gigantic building with magnificent stone faces, serves as Angkor Thom's main entryway. The famous peaceful faces staring in four directions depict Bodhisattva Avalokiteshvara and provide a sense of divine protection as you enter the old city.

Bayon Temple:

The magnificent Bayon Temple, located in the middle of Angkor Thom, is known for its enigmatic smiling faces carved into gigantic stone towers. The temple's center location in Angkor Thom represents the meeting of heaven and earth, and its elaborate carvings reflect scenes from daily life, mythology, and the splendor of the Khmer court.

Baphuon:

The Baphuon, located adjacent to Bayon, is a large three-tiered temple-mountain dedicated to the Hindu god Shiva. It represents Mount Meru, the mythological abode of the gods. Ascend its lofty walkways to get panoramic views of Angkor Thom.

Terrace of Elephants:

This spectacular terrace was used as a viewing platform for royal rituals and processions. The elaborate carvings of elephants and garudas demonstrate the Khmer Empire's military strength and cultural refinement.

The Terrace of the Leper King

The Terrace of the Leper King, named for the statue at its center, is adorned with elaborate sculptures and bas-reliefs. The terrace is said to reflect the soul's journey into the afterlife.

Must-See Sights in Angkor Thom

1. Bayon Temple Faces

Admire the enigmatic stone faces of Bayon, each delicately sculpted with a tranquil grin. Wander through the temple's labyrinthine halls and up its steep staircases to get a closer look at these captivating faces.

2. Southgate Faces:

As you enter Angkor Thom via the South Gate, take a minute to see the towering stone faces that flank the bridge. The South Gate faces represent the beneficent Bodhisattva Avalokiteshvara, who welcomes travelers into the ancient city.

3. Baphuon Central Tower:

Climb to the pinnacle of the Baphuon for amazing views of Angkor Thom. The restoration of the central tower demonstrates the painstaking efforts made to preserve and exhibit the Khmer Empire's architectural beauty.

4. Terrace of the Elephant Carvings:

Explore the Terrace of the Elephants' intricate sculptures, which portray elephants, mythical creatures, and scenes from regal processions. The terrace reveals significant details about the Khmer civilization's cultural and military capabilities.

5. Terrace of the Leper King Statue.

Admire the figure at the center of the Terrace of the Leper ruler, which is thought to depict either the Khmer ruler or Yama, the god of death. The terrace's exquisite sculptures tell a story about spiritual significance and artistic excellence.

No. 5.5 Banteay Srei

The Pink Sandstone Gem

Banteay Srei, popularly known as the "Citadel of Women," is a gem among Angkor temples, distinguished by its delicate carvings and usage of pink sandstone. While lower in size than some of its peers, Banteay Srei is a marvel of Khmer creativity, displaying great craftsmanship and attention to detail.

Historical significance:

Banteay Srei was built in the tenth century and is dedicated to the Hindu god Shiva. Its modest size betrays the incredible complexity of its carvings, demonstrating the mastery of Khmer artists of the

Angkor period.

Architectural marvels:

The temple's pink sandstone walls are embellished with beautiful bas-reliefs depicting Hindu mythology and daily life. The carvings are surprisingly well-preserved, displaying intricate intricacies and skilled craftsmanship.

Day Trip to the Intricate Temple:

Traveling to Banteay Srei:

To get to Banteay Srei, take a picturesque route through Cambodian countryside. The temple is located around 25 kilometers northeast of the main Angkor complex. The drive provides glimpses into rural life, with rice paddies, traditional wooden cottages, and palm palms bordering the road.

Must-see Features:

1. Central Sanctuary:

Admire the main sanctuary, which features beautiful carvings and pink sandstone walls.

Explore the sanctuary's three major towers, each with its own portrayal of deities and legendary figures.

2.Bibliography and Surrounding Structures:

Discover the libraries flanking the center temple, each with intricate carvings.

Explore the outer courtyards, where free-standing structures feature more bas-reliefs and intricate decorations.

3. The Lotus Pond and Reflections:

Photograph the temple's reflection in a nearby lotus pond, preferably in the mellow light of early morning or late afternoon.

The pond lends a peaceful and scenic element to the overall atmosphere of Banteay Srei.

Visitor Tips:

Entrance price: Banteay Srei charges a separate entrance price from the main Angkor complex, so check for any updated ticket information.

Guided Tours: Speak with local guides who can explain the temple's history, architectural significance, and the stories behind the beautiful sculptures.

Conservation Efforts: Because of the temple's delicate sandstone carvings, visitors are requested to follow preservation rules to ensure the temple's artistic treasures are preserved for future generations.

Finally, a visit to Angkor Thom and Banteay Srei provides a fascinating glimpse into the heart of Khmer culture. The grandeur and architectural splendor of Angkor Thom, together with the exquisite workmanship of Banteay Srei, offer a full look at Cambodia's rich history and cultural legacy. Whether admiring the smiling faces of Bayon or the detailed sculptures of Banteay Srei, each temple inside the Angkor complex contributes a distinct chapter to the story of this ancient empire.

5.6 Phnom Bakheng

Sunset View and Serenity

Phnom Bakheng, a venerated temple perched atop a hill within the Angkor Archaeological Park, provides amazing sunset views as well as a quiet escape into Cambodia's ancient history. This temple, built in the late ninth century during King Yasovarman I's reign, predates Angkor Wat and is one of the Angkor complex's oldest structures.

Climbing the Temple for panoramic views:

Sunset Views:

Phnom Bakheng is famous for offering one of the most beautiful sunset views in Angkor. As the day comes to an end, visitors climb the temple to see the shifting colors of the sky and the silhouette of Angkor Wat in the distance. The panoramic views create a magnificent environment, transforming the temple into a viewing platform for capturing the grandeur of the surrounding area.

Climbing Tips:

1. Early Arrival: Due to its popularity, particularly at sunset, consider arriving early to obtain a good place. The temple has a limited capacity, so arriving early allows for a more comfortable and enjoyable visit.

2. Sturdy Footwear: The trek to the top of Phnom Bakheng requires navigating steep and narrow stairs. To make it easier to climb the steps, choose comfortable, solid footwear.

3. Camera Ready: Bring a camera to record the breathtaking sunset views. The interplay of light and shadow on the old temple structures creates a magnificent scene.

4. Conservation Awareness: As with all temples in Angkor, follow conservation standards. Stay on designated routes and avoid touching carvings or structures to help preserve this historic monument.

5.7 Terrace of Elephants

Historical Significance, Architecture

The Terrace of the Elephants, a 350-meter-long sandstone platform, is a notable architectural and historical landmark in the Angkor Thom complex. This terrace, built by King Jayavarman VII in the late 12th century, was used as a grandstand for public rituals like as military parades and royal processions.

Insightful Guided Tours:

Historical significance:

1. Military Ceremonies: The terrace's name comes from the elaborate carvings of elephants on the walls. These carvings portray ceremonial military processions, symbolizing the Khmer Empire's might.

2. Architectural Details: The terrace is embellished with intricate carvings depicting warriors, horses, mythical entities, and different scenes from daily life. The carvings provide insight into the Khmer Empire's military might and cultural refinement.

Architecture:

1. Raised Platform: The elevated platform includes a central stairway that leads to the lower courtyard. This design emphasizes the terrace's use as a ceremonial stage for the king and his court.

2. Elephant Carvings: The prominent carvings of elephants, each meticulously embellished with ceremonial trappings, demonstrate the Khmer Empire's respect for these powerful beasts.

3. Guardians and Deities: Beyond the elephants, the terrace is decorated with carvings of guardian figures, celestial beings, and other Hindu deities that reflect the religious and cultural influences of the time.

Insightful Guided Tours

Consider taking a guided tour to fully appreciate the Terrace of the Elephants' historical and architectural significance:

Local Guides: Experienced local guides may provide detailed explanations of the carvings, historical events, and cultural background surrounding the terrace.

Audio tours: Some visitors choose audio tours, which allow them to explore the terrace at their own speed while obtaining thorough commentary on its attractions.

Group Tours: Participating in a guided group tour provides an engaging experience, allowing for questions and debates regarding the terrace's significance in Khmer history.

Visitor Tips:

1. Entrance Information: The Terrace of the Elephants is accessible with a valid Angkor Pass, which allows access to the Angkor Thom complex.

2. Time of Visit: Plan your visit for early morning or late afternoon, when the soft sunshine improves the visibility of the carvings and creates a more comfortable environment.

3. Conservation Awareness: Follow conservation guidelines by not touching carvings and remaining on authorized walkways. Maintain the historical integrity of this beautiful terrace.

5.8 Preah Khan

Exploring the Royal Sword Temple.

Preah Khan, also known as the "Royal Sword Temple," is hidden in the dense woods northeast of Angkor Thom. It is a gigantic tangle of hallways, courtyards, and finely carved temples. In the 12th century, King Jayavarman VII commissioned this temple to operate as a multifarious monastery complex, comprising not just religious areas but also monks' apartments and administrative facilities.

Hidden Gems and Less-Known Areas:

Layout and Significance:

1. Grand Entrance: Preah Khan greets visitors with beautiful carvings and devatas (divine female figures). The entrance establishes the tone for the architectural beauty within.

2. Central Sanctuary: The heart of Preah Khan is the central sanctuary, which is decorated with the four-faced Bodhisattva Avalokiteshvara, a symbol of compassion. This temple was dedicated to the king's father.

3. Hall of Dancers: Marvel at the Hall of Dancers, which features beautiful sculptures of celestial Apsara dancers that exemplify the Khmer Empire's creative flair.

4. Libraries and Shrines: Explore the temple grounds' various libraries and shrines, each of which reveals a particular facet of Khmer architecture and religious practice.

Hidden Gems:

1. Lintel Landscape: Notice the finely carved lintels illustrating mythological legends. These treasures are spread throughout Preah Khan and are sometimes overlooked by casual tourists.

2. Moss-Covered Ruins: Enjoy the peaceful atmosphere of moss-covered ruins, particularly in the soft light of sunrise or late afternoon. The mix of nature and old stones lends a mysterious quality to the shrine.

3. Northern Hall: Explore the lesser-known northern hall, which contains remarkable carvings and offers a peaceful space for contemplation.

4. West Prasat: Visit the West Prasat, an elevated platform that provides panoramic views of the surrounding jungle. This less-frequented location offers a peaceful respite.

Visitor Tips:

1. Guided Tours: Hire a qualified local guide to explain the historical and architectural significance of Preah Khan. Guides can show you hidden corners and provide anecdotes that bring the temple to life.

2. Conservation Awareness: As with all Angkor temples, please follow conservation rules. Avoid touching the engravings, stay on designated routes, and help preserve this ancient place.

3. Early Exploration: For a more intimate experience, visit Preah Khan in the early morning, when the temple is bathed in soft light and the crowds are smaller.

No. 5.9 Tonle Sap Lake

Floating Villages and Boat Tours

Tonle Sap Lake, Southeast Asia's largest freshwater lake, is located just south of Siem Reap. This massive body of water is crucial to Cambodia's ecosystem, providing a unique way of life for many populations that live in floating villages along its banks.

Experience the Unique Ecosystem:

Floating villages:

1. Chong Khneas: Take a boat journey to Chong Khneas, one of the most accessible floating villages from Siem Reap. Observe stilted dwellings, floating schools, and markets as locals go about their everyday activities.

2.Kampong Phluk: Discover Kampong Phluk, a less touristy floating village famous for its stilted buildings surrounded by mangrove trees. During the wet season, water levels increase, allowing boats to pass across the flooded forest.

3. Kompong Khleang: For a more real experience, head to Kompong Khleang, where stilted buildings reach heights of up to ten meters. This village sheds light on the struggles and perseverance of communities adapting to the lake's ever-changing environment.

Boat Tours:

1. Sunset Cruises: Take a sunset cruise on Tonle Sap Lake, which offers a beautiful view as the sun sets below the horizon. The reflections on the calm waters create a peaceful and lovely scene.

2. Tonle Sap is a sanctuary for bird watchers. Bring binoculars to view diverse bird species, especially during the migratory season, when the lake serves as an important stopover for migratory birds.

3. Floating woods: During the rainy season, behold the rare occurrence of "floating forests." Trees submerged in water form an ethereal environment, allowing an insight into the lake's dynamic ecosystem.

Conservation Awareness:

1. Responsible Tourism: Look for tour operators who promote environmental sustainability and contribute to the well-being of their communities.

2. Support Local Economies: Buy locally manufactured handicrafts and products from the floating markets to help the lakeside villages support their lives.

3. Educational excursions: Consider excursions that provide information about Tonle Sap Lake's environmental challenges and current efforts to preserve its biodiversity.

Visitor Tips:

1. Boat Safety: Ensure that the boat operator follows safety guidelines. Life jackets should be given, and the boat must be in good condition.

2. Seasonal Considerations: The lake's water levels change dramatically between the dry and wet seasons. Plan your visit properly to see the different aspects of Tonle Sap depending on the time of year.

3. Local Etiquette: Follow the cultural standards of the floating communities. Seek permission before taking images, and treat the residents with respect.

Chapter 6: Specialized Traveler Guides

6.1 History Seekers

Delving Deeper into Angkor's Rich Past

For the avid history seeker, Angkor Wat is not merely a temple complex; it's a portal to an ancient civilization that flourished in the heart of Southeast Asia. Delving deeper into Angkor's rich past requires a curated approach, combining immersive experiences, expert-guided tours, and visits to museums that house the remnants of this remarkable era.

Recommended Tours:

1. Angkor Wat Sunrise Tour: Begin your historical journey with the iconic Angkor Wat sunrise tour. As the first light of dawn bathes the temple's intricate facades, you'll witness the awakening of a structure that has stood the test of centuries. Engage a knowledgeable guide to unravel the stories embedded in the bas-reliefs, depicting scenes from Hindu epics and daily Khmer life.

2. Angkor Thom Exploration: Traverse the grandeur of Angkor Thom, the last and most enduring capital city of the Khmer Empire. Visit Bayon with its enigmatic smiling faces, the Terrace of the Elephants, and the Terrace of the Leper King. Each site unveils a chapter of the empire's history, showcasing the grand architectural and artistic achievements of the Khmer people.

3. Ta Prohm, the Jungle Temple: Explore Ta Prohm, the jungle temple that has been left in a state of captivating ruin. The intertwining of massive tree roots with temple structures tells a tale of nature's reclamation. Guided tours provide insights into the conservation efforts to preserve the delicate balance between ancient ruins and the surrounding environment.

Museums to Visit:

1. Angkor National Museum: Located in Siem Reap, the Angkor National Museum serves as an excellent starting point for history enthusiasts. The museum's galleries house artifacts, multimedia presentations, and detailed exhibits that provide context to Angkor's historical and cultural significance.

2. Cambodian Landmine Museum and Relief Center: While not exclusively focused on Angkor, this museum near Siem Reap sheds light on Cambodia's more recent history, including the Khmer Rouge era. It serves as a poignant reminder of the country's resilience and ongoing efforts for landmine clearance.

3. Siem Reap War Museum: Explore Cambodia's modern history at the Siem Reap War Museum, which showcases military hardware, weaponry, and exhibitions related to Cambodia's tumultuous past. Gain a comprehensive understanding of the challenges faced by the nation.

Visitor Tips:

1. Expert Guides: Invest in guided tours with experts well-versed in Khmer history. Their narratives will provide context and a deeper understanding of the cultural and historical nuances.

2. Sunrise and Sunset: Take advantage of the serene moments during sunrise and sunset. The play of light on the temples adds a mystical dimension to your historical exploration.

3. Conservation Awareness: Respect conservation guidelines when visiting temples. Avoid touching carvings, stay on designated paths, and contribute to the preservation of these invaluable historical sites.

4. Extended Stay: Consider an extended stay to absorb the richness of Angkor's history fully. Multiple days allow for a more leisurely exploration and a comprehensive appreciation of the diverse temple complexes.

6.2 Adventure Seekers

Thrilling Activities and Outdoor Excursions

For the adventure seeker, Angkor Wat is not just an archaeological wonder; it's a playground for thrilling activities and outdoor excursions. From soaring through the treetops on zip lines to cycling through ancient ruins and trekking along scenic trails, Angkor offers an adrenaline-pumping experience amidst its historical grandeur.

Zip-lining Adventure:

Discover a unique perspective of the Angkor Archaeological Park by embarking on a zip-lining adventure. Several companies offer exhilarating zip-line experiences that take you through the lush jungles surrounding Angkor. Imagine gliding above the towering trees, catching glimpses of ancient temples below. It's a heart-pounding yet awe-inspiring way to appreciate the sheer scale and beauty of this UNESCO World Heritage site.

Cycling Expeditions:

Explore Angkor's vast complex on two wheels with cycling

expeditions that cater to all fitness levels. Rent a bike or join a guided cycling tour to navigate the labyrinthine paths connecting the temples. Feel the wind in your hair as you pedal past iconic structures like Angkor Wat, Bayon, and Ta Prohm. Cycling provides a flexible and immersive way to delve into the details of each temple while enjoying the natural surroundings.

Hiking Trails:

For those who prefer a slower pace on foot, Angkor offers enchanting hiking trails that lead you through less-explored areas. Immerse yourself in the tranquility of the Cambodian countryside as you meander along paths flanked by ancient trees and hidden temples. Guided hiking tours can take you to remote temples, offering a more intimate experience away from the crowds.

Zip-lining Adventures:

1. Flight of the Gibbon: Experience the thrill of zip-lining with

Flight of the Gibbon, an eco-adventure company that combines adrenaline-pumping activities with a focus on conservation. Soar through the jungle, taking in panoramic views of the temples and surrounding greenery.

2. Angkor Zipline: Another popular choice is Angkor Zipline, offering a series of zip lines and sky bridges. The course is designed to provide an exciting adventure while maintaining a commitment to environmental sustainability.

Cycling Expeditions:

1. Angkor Cycling Tour: Join a guided cycling tour that takes you on a scenic route through the Angkor complex. Explore the major temples and hidden gems, with knowledgeable guides sharing insights into the historical and cultural significance of each site.

2. Self-Guided Bike Rental: For independent adventurers, opt for self-guided bike rentals available in Siem Reap. Armed with a map and a sense of exploration, you can create your own itinerary and pedal at your own pace.

Hiking Trails:

1.Kulen Mountain Trails: Consider hiking trails around Phnom Kulen, a sacred mountain located about 40 kilometers from Siem Reap. The trails lead to waterfalls, ancient ruins, and a reclining Buddha statue, providing a unique blend of nature and history.

2. Angkor Remote Temples Trek: Engage in an Angkor remote temples trek, exploring less-visited temples such as Beng Mealea and Koh Ker. These sites offer a sense of adventure, with overgrown vegetation and a feeling of discovering hidden treasures.

Visitor Tips:

1. Safety First: Prioritize safety when engaging in adventure activities. Choose reputable operators with certified equipment and experienced guides.

2. Weather Considerations: Be mindful of the weather, especially during the hot season. Stay hydrated, wear appropriate clothing, and plan activities for the cooler parts of the day.

3. Fitness Levels: Select activities based on your fitness levels and preferences. Whether you choose zip-lining, cycling, or hiking, there are options for varying levels of physical exertion.

4. Accommodation Choices: Consider staying in Siem Reap, where you'll find a range of accommodation options catering to adventure seekers. From budget-friendly hostels to comfortable hotels, there's something for every traveler.

6.3 Cruise Tours

Navigating Angkor Wat by Water

For those seeking a more leisurely exploration of Angkor Wat, the ancient wonders of Cambodia can be admirably discovered by water. Cruise tours offer a unique perspective, allowing travelers to meander along waterways, witness the majestic temples from the comfort of a boat, and experience the serene beauty that envelops this historic landscape.

Cruise Options:

1. Tonle Sap Lake Cruises: Begin your aquatic adventure with a cruise on Tonle Sap Lake, the largest lake in Southeast Asia. These cruises often depart from the floating village of Chong Khneas and take you on a captivating journey through the expansive lake, passing floating houses, stilted communities, and lush landscapes. The lake's proximity to Angkor Wat ensures that you'll enjoy stunning views of the temples from a unique vantage point.

2. Angkor Thom Moat Cruises: Experience the grandeur of Angkor Thom from the tranquility of its ancient moat. Cruise tours along the moat provide a distinct perspective of the iconic Bayon Temple, the Terrace of the Elephants, and the Terrace of the Leper King. As you gently glide on the water, you'll witness the intricate details of these architectural marvels framed by the reflection in the moat.

3. Lotus Pond Cruises: Delight in the beauty of the Lotus Pond, a serene body of water nestled within the Angkor Thom complex. Cruise tours on the Lotus Pond offer a peaceful and picturesque journey, allowing you to appreciate the surrounding temples, including the enchanting Baphuon and Phimeanakas.

Sightseeing from the River:

1. Floating Village Views: Tonle Sap Lake cruises provide a captivating glimpse into the unique lifestyle of floating villages. Witness the daily activities of locals as you cruise past floating schools, markets, and homes, gaining insights into the symbiotic relationship between communities and the lake.

2. Sunset on the Moat: Opt for a cruise during the golden hour to experience the magic of Angkor Thom at sunset. The temples, bathed in the warm hues of the setting sun, create a mesmerizing scene reflected on the moat's calm waters. It's an ideal setting for capturing breathtaking photographs.

3. Wildlife Spotting: Tonle Sap Lake is renowned for its diverse ecosystem. Keep an eye out for migratory birds, especially during the bird-watching season. The lake's floating forests and wetlands are home to a variety of avian species, providing an opportunity for nature enthusiasts to indulge in wildlife spotting.

Cruise Tour Companies:

1. Sokha Cruises: Offering a range of cruises on Tonle Sap Lake, Sokha Cruises provides a luxurious experience with comfortable boats and knowledgeable guides. Choose from sunrise, sunset, or full-day cruises to tailor your Angkor Wat exploration.

2. Angkor Gondola Boat Tour: Experience the tranquility of the Lotus Pond with Angkor Gondola Boat Tour. Their traditional wooden boats offer a serene journey through the ancient moat, providing an intimate encounter with the temples of Angkor Thom.

Visitor Tips:

1. Comfortable Attire: Wear comfortable clothing and footwear suitable for a leisurely cruise. Sunscreen and a hat are advisable to protect against the sun.

2. Photography Gear: Bring a camera to capture the stunning landscapes and temple reflections. A telephoto lens may be handy for wildlife and architectural details.

3. Booking in Advance: Especially during peak tourist seasons, consider booking your cruise in advance to secure your preferred timing and ensure availability.

4. Accommodation Choices: Choose accommodation in Siem Reap, where you'll find a variety of options catering to different budgets. The town's central location provides easy access to both Angkor Wat and embarkation points for cruise tours.

6.4 Vacations and Relaxation

Leisurely Strolls and Relaxing Activities

While Angkor Wat is renowned for its historical significance, it also offers an idyllic setting for those seeking vacations centered around relaxation and tranquility. Embrace leisurely strolls through ancient temple complexes, partake in calming activities, and discover spa retreats that provide a perfect blend of cultural exploration and rejuvenation.

Leisurely Strolls:

1. Angkor Wat Gardens: Take unhurried strolls through the meticulously landscaped gardens surrounding Angkor Wat. The juxtaposition of lush greenery against the intricate architecture creates a serene atmosphere, perfect for leisurely exploration and contemplation.

2. Bakheng Hill Sunset Stroll: Embark on a late afternoon stroll up Bakheng Hill to witness a breathtaking sunset over Angkor Wat. The leisurely ascent allows you to absorb the changing colors of the sky and the ancient temples below.

3. South Gate of Angkor Thom: Wander through the South Gate of Angkor Thom, adorned with serene stone faces. The pathway leading to the Bayon Temple provides a calming environment, with the gentle rustling of leaves and the occasional sound of temple bells.

Relaxing Activities:

1. Lotus Pond Meditation: Find solace at the Lotus Pond within the Angkor Thom complex. Engage in meditation or simply revel in the peaceful surroundings. The reflection of ancient temples on the tranquil water surface adds to the meditative ambiance.

2. Traditional Apsara Dance Performances: Unwind in the evening with traditional Apsara dance performances. Many hotels and restaurants in Siem Reap offer these cultural displays, providing a soothing way to end your day.

2. **Countryside Bicycle Rides:** Explore the picturesque Cambodian countryside on a leisurely bicycle ride. Cycle along the outskirts of Siem Reap, passing through rice fields and traditional villages, creating a sense of serenity far from the bustling crowds.

Spa Recommendations:

1. Bodia Spa: Indulge in a pampering experience at Bodia Spa, known for its holistic approach to well-being. Located in the heart of Siem Reap, Bodia Spa offers a range of traditional Khmer massages, rejuvenating facials, and wellness treatments.

2. Frangipani Spa: Discover tranquility at Frangipani Spa, nestled in a tropical garden setting. Choose from a menu of massages and spa packages designed to relax both the body and mind. The soothing ambiance enhances the overall spa experience.

3. Navutu Dreams Resort & Wellness Retreat: For those seeking an immersive wellness retreat, consider Navutu Dreams. This resort not only offers luxurious accommodation but also a wellness center with yoga classes, spa treatments, and detox programs.

Quiet Corners:

1. Neak Pean Temple: Escape the crowds and discover the secluded Neak Pean Temple, situated on an artificial island within a serene reservoir. The tranquility of this spot makes it an ideal location for quiet contemplation and relaxation.

2. Phimeanakas Temple: Visit Phimeanakas, a temple tucked away within the Royal Palace enclosure. Its off-the-beaten-path location often results in a more peaceful atmosphere, allowing visitors to appreciate the architectural beauty in solitude.

3. Terrace of the Leper King: Explore the Terrace of the Leper King, a less frequented area within Angkor Thom. The intricate carvings and historical significance of this site create a tranquil setting for reflection and relaxation.

Visitor Tips:

1. Cultural Etiquette: Respect the cultural and spiritual significance of the temples. Speak in hushed tones and maintain a peaceful demeanor, especially in quieter areas.

2. Appropriate Attire: Wear comfortable and modest clothing, especially when exploring temples. This ensures both cultural sensitivity and personal comfort.

3. Early Mornings: Consider early morning visits to popular sites to experience a quieter atmosphere and witness the temples in the soft morning light.

4. Accommodation Choices: Select accommodations that prioritize relaxation, such as boutique hotels or resorts with lush gardens. Siem Reap offers a range of options to suit various preferences and budgets.

6.5 Returning Visitors

Off-the-Beaten-Path Experiences

For those returning to the enchanting realm of Angkor Wat, the prospect of delving deeper into its mysteries beckons. Beyond the well-trodden paths lie hidden gems and lesser-known attractions that promise a renewed sense of discovery. Returning visitors have the opportunity to unveil the secrets of Angkor, uncovering off-the-beaten-path experiences that showcase the breadth and depth of Cambodia's cultural heritage.

Hidden Gems and Lesser-Known Attractions:

1. Beng Mealea Temple: Located about 40 kilometers east of the main Angkor complex, Beng Mealea Temple stands as a testament to nature's reclamation. Often referred to as the "Jungle Temple," it offers a captivating blend of ancient ruins entwined with the embrace of lush vegetation. Exploring Beng Mealea provides a sense of adventure and discovery as you navigate through collapsed galleries and intricate stone carvings.

2. Koh Ker: Venture further afield to the archaeological site of Koh Ker, approximately 120 kilometers northeast of Siem Reap. This remote complex is home to the iconic Prasat Thom pyramid, providing a unique perspective on Khmer architecture. The journey to Koh Ker offers an immersive experience of Cambodia's countryside, and the site itself is a captivating exploration of temples surrounded by a serene forest.

3. Phnom Kulen: Consider a visit to Phnom Kulen, a sacred mountain range revered for its cultural and historical significance. Discover hidden waterfalls, ancient temple ruins, and a reclining Buddha statue. The peaceful atmosphere of Phnom Kulen provides a serene contrast to the bustling crowds at more popular Angkor sites.

Unique Experiences for Returning Visitors:

1. Sunrise at Srah Srang: While Angkor Wat's sunrise is iconic, returning visitors can seek a quieter alternative at Srah Srang, the Royal Bath. The tranquil reservoir offers a serene setting to witness the dawn, with the surrounding temples casting reflections on the calm waters.

2. Lotus Farm Exploration: Engage in a unique experience by exploring the lotus farms near Tonle Sap Lake. Witness the traditional harvesting of lotus flowers, an essential aspect of Cambodian culture. The vibrant colors and intricate process make for a fascinating and off-the-beaten-path excursion.

3. Community-based Tourism: Support community-based tourism initiatives around Siem Reap. These programs provide insight into local life, traditional crafts, and community development projects. Participating in homestays or guided village tours allows returning visitors to contribute to the local economy while experiencing authentic Cambodian hospitality.

Accommodation Options for Returning Visitors:

1. Heritage Suites Hotel: Nestled in a tropical garden setting, Heritage Suites Hotel offers a luxurious retreat with Khmer-inspired design. The boutique hotel provides an intimate and serene atmosphere, allowing returning visitors to unwind in elegance.

2. Phum Baitang: Experience a blend of luxury and authenticity at Phum Baitang, a five-star resort surrounded by rice paddies and palm trees. The stilted villas offer a tranquil escape, and the resort's commitment to sustainability adds an eco-friendly touch to the stay.

3. Amansara: For a truly exclusive experience, consider Amansara, a resort set in a historic villa once used by King Norodom Sihanouk. The resort provides personalized service and a sophisticated ambiance, catering to discerning travelers seeking a refined retreat.

Visitor Tips:

1. Flexible Itineraries: Returning visitors should consider flexible itineraries to allow for spontaneous exploration. Embrace the opportunity to revisit favorite sites while leaving room for new discoveries.

2. Local Guides: Engage local guides who can offer insights into lesser-known attractions and share personal stories about the region's history and culture.

3. Cultural Respect: As returning visitors explore off-the-beaten-path locations, maintaining respect for cultural and environmental preservation is crucial. Adhere to guidelines and regulations to ensure the continued protection of these hidden gems.

4. Transportation Options: Consider various transportation options, such as hiring a private driver or exploring by bicycle, to access more remote sites comfortably.

Chapter 7: What to Do and Not to Do

7.1 Respecting Culture and Customs

Cultural Sensitivity Tips:

Traveling to Angkor Wat involves more than just admiring old structures; it also requires a deep appreciation for Cambodia's diverse culture and customs. Adhering to cultural sensitivity guidelines offers a meaningful and peaceful experience for both visitors and local residents.

Cultural Sensitivity Tip:

1. Greetings and gestures:

customary Greetings: Accept the customary Cambodian greeting, the Sampeah. Place your palms together in a prayer-like position and bow gently. This kind greeting is really appreciated.

Use of Hands: Do not point your feet at people or religious items. Additionally, using your left hand for gestures or passing goods is considered disrespectful.

2. Respectful Monks:

Modesty in Presence: Use caution when in the presence of Buddhist monks. Avoid establishing physical contact and keep a respectful distance during religious events or when monks are praying.

3. Photographic Etiquette:

Request Permission: Always ask permission before photographing anybody, especially monks or locals. Some people may prefer not to be photographed, and it is important to respect their desires.

Temples & Religious Sites: Follow the rules for photography within temples. Flash photography may be forbidden in certain situations, so follow these recommendations.

4. Conservative Dress Code

Suitable Attire: When visiting temples and religious sites, dress modestly. Both males and females should cover their shoulders and knees. Wearing attire that shows too much skin could be deemed impolite.

Proper Attire and Behavior at Temples

appropriate attire:

1. Shoulders and Knees Covered: When entering temples, please wear attire that covers your shoulders and knees. Both men and women should follow this dress code out of respect for the site's holiness.

2. Remove hats and shoes.

Hats: As a sign of respect, remove your hats and headwear before entering temple structures.

Shoes: Remove your shoes when entering temple interiors. This practice is a traditional symbol of humility and cleanliness.

3. Quiet and Respectful Behavior:

Silence in Prayer settings: Keep a quiet demeanor while in prayer settings. Visitors to the temple are expected to speak quietly and move with reverence.

No Climbing or Touching: Please do not climb the temple

buildings or touch the carvings. The old buildings are fragile, and physical contact might hasten their decay.

4. Participation at Ceremonies:

Observation: If a religious ceremony is currently taking place, keep a respectful distance and observe discreetly. Do not disrupt the service by strolling through the congregation.

Visitor Tips:

1.Educate Yourself: Before visiting Cambodia, become acquainted with the country's customs and cultural practices. Understanding local traditions improves the quality of your interactions in the community.

2.Pack appropriately: Bring clothing that follows the strict dress requirement required at religious places. Lightweight, breathable textiles are best suited to Cambodia's tropical climate.

3. Guided Tours: Consider hiring a local guide who can explain cultural intricacies and advise on acceptable behavior. They can help you comprehend the historical and cultural significance of the sites.

4. Language Courtesy: Learn some basic Khmer phrases like greetings and appreciation. Locals enjoy visitors who try to speak in their language.

5.Responsible tourist: Follow responsible tourist practices. Avoid littering, defacing monuments, and any other behaviors that could affect the region's cultural and natural assets.

7.2: Conservation and Sustainability

Eco-Friendly Practices in Responsible Tourism

A trip to Angkor Wat is more than just seeing historical landmarks; it's also an opportunity to practice responsible tourism. Adopting eco-friendly techniques and adhering to sustainability principles helps to preserve the region's natural and cultural assets.

Eco-friendly Practices:

1. Sustainable Transport:

Bicycling: Explore the temple complex by bicycle, reducing your carbon impact and supporting a healthier way of transportation.

Electric Tuk-tuks: Use electric tuk-tuks when possible. These automobiles contribute less to air pollution than regular ones.

2. Waste reduction:

Reusable Water Bottles: Carry a reusable water bottle to help reduce single-use plastic waste. Refill stations are accessible throughout the Angkor complex.

Pack Out What You Bring In: Follow the "Leave No Trace" philosophy and take your rubbish with you. Trash should be disposed of responsibly, and if possible, participate in clean-up projects.

3. Support Local and Sustainable Tourism.

Local Markets: Buy items at local markets to help Cambodian artists earn a living.

Eco-Friendly Tours: Select tour companies that are committed to sustainable methods. Eco-friendly excursions frequently focus on reducing environmental effect and supporting local conservation efforts.

Leave No Trace Principles

The Principles for Responsible Tourism:

1. Plan and Prepare:

Research Regulations: Become acquainted with Angkor's norms and regulations. Knowing what to do and what not to do helps you explore responsibly.

Weather Considerations: Be mindful of weather conditions and their effects on the environment. Some regions may become more vulnerable to foot traffic during the wet season.

2. Follow Designated Paths:

Preserve Flora and Fauna: Follow marked trails and designated paths to avoid trampling on delicate vegetation. Respecting the natural environment helps to maintain the ecological equilibrium.

3. Proper Disposal of Waste:

Carry Out What You Carry In: Avoid leaving any waste behind, including biodegradable products. Place rubbish in appropriate bins or carry it with you until proper disposal is available.

4. Respect the Wildlife:

Observe from a distance: Do not approach or disturb wildlife. Maintain a respectful distance so that animals can behave naturally.

5. Minimize Campfire Impact:

Use Designated Areas: If camping is in your plan, use existing fire pits. To conserve the landscape, avoid building new fire locations.

6. Be considerate to other visitors:

Respect Quiet Zones: Certain areas may be designated as quiet zones or sacred spaces. Follow these guidelines to ensure a tranquil and meditative environment for all visitors.

7. Educate others:

Share Conservation Practices: Encourage other travelers to follow responsible tourism practices. You may help to save Angkor Wat for future generations by raising awareness about the site.

7.3 Local Etiquette

Interacting with locals

Engaging with the local communities enriches your Angkor Wat experience. Understanding Cambodian customs and exhibiting polite behavior promotes better relationships with the people who live in this region.

Interacting with locals:

1. Warm greetings

grin and Sampeah: Greet locals with a friendly grin and a traditional Cambodian Sampeah. This considerate gesture fosters a nice environment.

2. Learn basic Khmer phrases:

Greetings: Learn common Khmer greetings like "Chum reap suor" (Hello) and "Orsas suor sdei" (Goodbye). Locals enjoy visitors who try to speak in their language.

3. Ask permission before photographing:

Respect Privacy: Always obtain permission before photographing residents. Some people may prefer not to be photographed, particularly in rural or traditional settings.

4. Show Respect for Local Traditions:

Ceremonies and celebrations: If you come across any local ceremonies or celebrations, be respectful. Avoid interrupting religious or cultural practices.

Understanding Cambodian Customs.

Key Customs to Be Mindful of:

1. Gift-giving Etiquette:

Present with Both Hands: Show respect by offering or receiving gifts with both hands. It is usual to open gifts in secret.

2. Remove Your Shoes Before Entering Homes:

Cultural Significance: When entering someone's home or specific institutions, take off your shoes. This practice is based on cultural and religious traditions.

3. Respect the Elders:

Use Proper Titles: Address seniors using proper titles such as "Lok" for older men and "Lok Srey" for elderly ladies. This reflects a cultural emphasis on respect for the elderly.

4. Conservative Dress for Traditional Settings:

Cover your shoulders and knees: When visiting traditional or rural areas, dress conservatively. Covering the shoulders and knees is frequently appreciated.

Visitor Tips:

1.Cultural Sensitivity Training: To obtain a better understanding of Cambodian cultures, consider taking cultural sensitivity classes or researching them before your visit.

2. Local Guides: Use local guides to create a more immersive experience. They can provide useful information about local customs and traditions.

3. Support Local Businesses: Choose local restaurants, markets, and businesses to help the local economy directly. This ensures that your tourism funds benefit the community.

4. Be Open to Learning: Seize the opportunity to learn about Cambodia's history, customs, and way of life. Approach contacts with an open mind and genuine interest in order to develop healthy relationships.

7.4 Safety and Health Tips:

Remaining Healthy and Safe During Your Visit

When exploring Angkor Wat, it is critical to ensure your safety and well-being first. Familiarizing yourself with health guidelines, getting the proper immunizations, and bringing a well-stocked first-aid kit all help to ensure a safe and pleasurable visit.

Stay Healthy:

1. Vaccinations:

normal immunizations: Make sure your normal immunizations, including measles, mumps, rubella (MMR), diphtheria, tetanus, and pertussis (DTaP), are up to date.

Travel-Specific immunizations: Ask your doctor about travel-specific immunizations. Vaccinations against hepatitis A and B, typhoid fever, and Japanese encephalitis are frequently advised for visitors visiting Cambodia.

2. Prevention of Mosquito-Borne Diseases:

Malaria Prevention: Depending on the season and locations you intend to travel, malaria prophylaxis may be recommended. Consult your healthcare provider to choose the best antimalarial drug.

Insect Repellent: To avoid mosquito bites, use insect repellent containing DEET, especially around dawn and dusk, when mosquitoes are most active.

3. Safe Food and Water Practices:

Bottled Water: To prevent waterborne infections, drink bottled or boiling water. Before drinking bottled water, be sure the seal is not damaged.

Avoid Street Food: While street food may be enticing, take caution and seek meals from recognized locations to reduce your risk of foodborne disease.

4. Heat and sun protection:

Hydration: Cambodia's weather can be hot and humid. Maintain hydration by drinking plenty of water throughout the day.

Sunscreen: Use a high SPF sunscreen to protect your skin from the hot tropical sun. Wearing a hat and lightweight, long-sleeved clothing also helps to avoid sunburn.

Vaccines and First Aid Supplies

Requirements for Your Health and Safety:

1. First Aid Kit:

Basic prescriptions: Keep a first-aid kit stocked with pain relievers, antidiarrheal medication, and any prescription prescriptions you take on a daily basis.

Bandages and Disinfectants: Bring adhesive bandages, antiseptic wipes, and any other wound-care materials.

bug Bite Relief: Carry ointment or lotion to treat bug bites and stings.

2. Health insurance:

Comprehensive Coverage: Get travel insurance that covers medical emergencies, including evacuation if necessary. Ensure that your insurance covers the activities you intend to participate in, such as hiking or adventure sports.

3. Emergency Contacts:

Local Emergency Numbers: Get to know your local emergency numbers, as well as the contact information for the nearest hospital or medical facility.

Embassy or Consulate: Save the contact information for your country's embassy or consulate in Cambodia in case of an emergency.

4. General Safety Tip:

Traffic Awareness: Be cautious when crossing roads because traffic can be busy. Use designated crosswalks and remain mindful of local traffic patterns.

Secure Valuables: Keep your items safe to prevent theft. Use a money belt or neck pouch to carry critical stuff, and be aware of your surroundings.

Emergency pack: Pack a compact emergency pack with necessities such as a flashlight, whistle, and basic tools.

5. COVID-19 precautions:

Mask and Sanitizers: Comply with any COVID-19 rules and regulations in effect. Carry masks and hand sanitizers for personal protection.

Visitor Tip:

1.Consult a Healthcare Professional: Before your journey, consult a healthcare professional about immunizations, health precautions, and any special medical concerns based on your personal health history.

2. Research healthcare facilities:

Medical Facility Location: Determine the proximity of medical facilities to your lodging and key tourist attractions.

Pharmacy Locations: Locate pharmacies where you can purchase over-the-counter drugs and basic medical supplies.

3. Stay informed:

Local Health Notices: Stay current on any local health notices or warnings. For updates during your stay, contact local authorities or your embassy.

4. Travel responsibly:

Respect COVID-19 standards: Follow COVID-19 standards, such as wearing masks and exercising social distancing, to protect yourself and others.

By putting your health and safety first, you can have a more enjoyable time while enjoying the delights of Angkor Wat. Responsible travel practices, together with preparation and awareness, help to create a memorable experience that promotes well-being.

7.5 Shopping and souvenirs.

Where to Find Authentic Souvenirs

Exploring the streets and stores surrounding Angkor Wat offers a unique opportunity to bring home original Cambodian goods. Here's a how-to guide for locating true treasures that reflect the region's unique cultural tapestry.

1. Old Market (Phsar Chas):

Location: Old Market, located in Siem Reap, is a thriving marketplace for local items and souvenirs.

What to Look for: Discover traditional Cambodian crafts, silk scarves, handmade textiles, and elaborately carved wooden pieces.

Bargaining Tips: Bargaining is usual, but it should be done with respect. Begin with a polite negotiation, aiming for a price that both you and the vendor consider reasonable.

2. Angkor Night Market:

Location: Adjacent to the Old Market, the Angkor Night Market opens in the evening and provides a colorful shopping experience.

What to Look for: Browse around stalls selling homemade items, artwork, apparel, and one-of-a-kind jewelry. Many products are handcrafted by local craftsmen.

Bargaining Tips: Practice polite negotiating, but keep in mind that developing a rapport with the dealer can result in better deals.

3. Artisan Angkor:

Location: This social enterprise operates workshops and a boutique near Angkor Wat.

What to Look for: Artisans Angkor specializes on high-quality Cambodian craftsmanship, such as silk items, stone and wood carvings, and silverware.

Bargaining Tips: Prices may be fixed, but you can look for package offers or inquire about any current discounts.

4. Psar Leu Market:

Location: Psar Leu Market, located in the middle of Siem Reap, is the area's main market.

What to Look for: From local food and fresh produce to clothing and traditional crafts, this market provides a variety shopping experience.

Bargaining Tips: Negotiate firmly, and consider purchasing in bulk for better rates on specific items.

5. The Cambodian Landmine Museum and Relief Center:

Location: While the center is primarily a museum, it also has an on-site gift shop that contributes to its objective.

What to Look for: Purchase handcrafted items manufactured by landmine survivors, such as jewelry, textiles, and artwork.

Bargaining Tips: Prices may be marked, but ask about any specials or discounts for helping the center's mission.

Bargaining Techniques for Market Shopping

177

Negotiation is an important aspect of the Cambodian market experience. Follow these ideas to get the most of your shopping experience:

1. Begin Polite Conversations:

Friendly Greetings: Start with a friendly greeting and a courteous discussion with the dealer. Building a positive rapport sets the tone for negotiations.

2. Know the value:

Research Prices: Determine a general price range for the things you're interested in. This information gives you strength during negotiations.

3. Express Interest but Remain Indecisive:

Show curiosity: Demonstrate real curiosity in the product, but remain unsure at first. Vendors may offer better deals to close a sale.

4. Start Bargaining with a Counteroffer:

Counteroffer: When the vendor quotes a price, make a counteroffer that is lower than what you are willing to spend. This provides room for bargaining.

5. Remain respectful and friendly:

Smile and Negotiate: Maintain a nice tone during the bargaining process. A grin can go a long way towards getting a decent deal.

6. Be willing to walk away:

Walk Away Tactfully: If the vendor does not agree to your desired pricing, be prepared to walk away. This may persuade the seller to offer a lesser price.

7. Bundle Items for Discount:

Package Deals: If you're buying numerous goods from the same vendor, ask about a package bargain or if there are any other items they can include.

8. Respect local customs:

Cultural Sensitivity: Bargaining is a cultural tradition, but it must be done respectfully. Avoid being too harsh or insulting during negotiations.

9. Consider the vendor's perspective:

Fair Pricing: When looking for a good offer, consider fair pricing. Recognize that sales are the vendor's primary source of income.

10. Enjoy the process:

Have Fun: Bargaining is supposed to be a playful discussion. Enjoy the process, and remember to appreciate the quality and care that went into the things you are acquiring.

Exploring local marketplaces and using these negotiating methods allows you to not only buy unique goods but also participate in an engaging cultural experience, which characterizes the allure of shopping in Cambodia.

Chapter 8: Culinary Delights

8.1 Cambodian Cuisine

Explore the vivid and diverse Khmer cuisine and embark on a fascinating trip through Cambodia's flavors. Khmer cuisine, with its aromatic spices, fresh herbs, and unusual ingredients, provides a culinary experience that represents the region's rich cultural past.

A Culinary Journey of Local Flavors

1. Rice, a staple grain:

Foundation of Khmer Cuisine: Rice is the staple of Khmer meals, complementing nearly every dish.

Rice Dishes: Sample a variety of rice-based dishes, including steamed jasmine rice, savory fried rice, and warm rice porridge.

2. Fragrant spices and herbs:

Distinctive Flavors: Khmer cuisine is distinguished by the use of aromatic spices and fresh herbs, including lemongrass, galangal, turmeric, and kaffir lime leaves.

Balancing Sweet, Sour, Salty, and Spicy: A careful balance of sweet, sour, salty, and spicy flavors results in harmonious dishes that delight the taste receptors.

3. Fresh seafood delights:

plenty of Seafood: Cambodia's seaside location provides a plenty of fresh seafood. Enjoy delicious prawns, delicate squid, and tasty fish dishes.

Fish Amok: Fish amok is a traditional Khmer meal that contains delicate fish fillets stewed in a fragrant coconut curry sauce and steamed in banana leaves.

4. Exotic Fruits & Vegetables:

Tropical Bounty: Discover the wide variety of tropical fruits and vegetables available in Cambodia's marketplaces and street vendors. From delicious mangoes and lush papayas to crisp cucumbers and fragrant herbs, the possibilities are limitless.

Green Mango Salad: This refreshing and zesty Khmer meal combines shredded green mangoes, fresh herbs, peanuts, and a tangy dressing.

Must-Try Dishes and Street Food

1. Bai Sach Chrouk (Grilled Pork and Rice):

morning Favorite: Bai sach chrouk, a popular morning dish, contains thinly sliced grilled pork served over rice with pickled vegetables and a side of flavorful broth.

2. Nom Banh Chok (Khmer Noodle Soup):

Noodle Soup Delight: Nom banh chok is a classic Khmer noodle soup made from fresh rice noodles, fish stock, and a variety of fresh herbs and vegetables. It is often eaten as a hearty breakfast or lunch dish.

3. Loc Lac (Khmer beef stir-fry):

Savory Stir-Fry: Loc lac is a savory beef stir-fry dish that is marinated in soy sauce, oyster sauce, and garlic before being swiftly fried with onions, bell peppers, and tomatoes. It comes with a side of fresh lettuce leaves and a zesty dipping sauce.

4. Kuy Teav (Cambodian Noodle Soup):

Comfort in a Bowl: Kuy teav is a nourishing noodle soup made with thin rice noodles, soft chunks of pig or beef, and a fragrant broth infused with garlic, star anise, and cinnamon. It's a popular street food alternative, garnished with fresh herbs, bean sprouts, and lime.

5. Num Pang (a Cambodian sandwich):

Portable Delight: Num pang is Cambodia's version of a sandwich, usually constructed with a baguette filled with savory ingredients including grilled pork, pâté, pickled vegetables, fresh herbs, and spicy chili sauce. It's an easy and delicious option for on-the-go eating.

6. Street Food Delicacies

Explore Local Markets: Stroll through the lively streets of Cambodia's cities and towns to find a variety of street cuisine treats. From grilled meat and seafood skewers to crispy spring rolls and sweet delicacies like fried bananas and sticky rice sweets, there's something for everyone's taste.

Enjoy the exquisite flavors of Khmer food while exploring Cambodia's rich culinary environment. Whether you're eating traditional dishes in a local restaurant or sampling street food from a crowded market stall, every mouthful reflects the rich cultural legacy and lively tastes that define Khmer cuisine.

8.2 Dining Experiences.

Embark on a culinary excursion in Cambodia, where dining transcends simply nutrition and becomes a sensory voyage. Cambodia has a wide variety of dining alternatives to suit every taste, from unusual restaurants that redefine culinary experiences to calm sunset dinners at riverbank cafés.

Unique Restaurants and Dining Settings

1. Nestled In Nature:

Malis Restaurant, Siem Reap: Experience nature at Malis Restaurant in Siem Reap. Surrounded by lush vegetation, this institution serves traditional Khmer cuisine with a modern twist. Dine in attractive pavilions or open-air places to enhance your meal with a serene atmosphere.

2.Historical Ambience:

Sugar Palm, Phnom Penh: Discover Cambodia's culinary heritage at Sugar Palm in Phnom Penh. The restaurant, housed in a lovely colonial-era home, provides traditional Khmer cuisine passed down through generations. Enjoy your dinner in a nostalgic environment that honors the nation's cultural history.

3. Floating Dining:

Floating Village Restaurants, Tonle Sap Lake: For a really memorable experience, visit Tonle Sap Lake's floating towns. Enjoy freshly caught seafood while floating on the water, surrounded by beautiful scenery of floating houses and locals.

4. Sky High Dining:

Eclipse Sky Bar, Phnom Penh: Enhance your dining experience with Eclipse Sky Bar. Located on the 23rd level, this Phnom Penh rooftop restaurant provides panoramic views of the city skyline. Dine under the stars and enjoy a combination of world and Khmer flavors.

5. Culinary Art Show:

Marum, Siem Reap: Marum not only satisfies the palate but also contributes to a good cause. This restaurant, part of the TREE Alliance for Marginalized Youth, serves excellent cuisine made by culinary students. Witness the culinary arts in action while helping a worthwhile cause.

Sunset Dinners and Riverside Restaurants

1. In a Romantic Riverside Setting

Foreign Correspondents' Club (FCC), Phnom Penh: Spend a romantic evening by the river at the FCC in Phnom Penh. This historic site, which was formerly a meeting point for journalists, today provides a stunning backdrop for sunset dinners. Enjoy a variety menu while taking in the breathtaking views of the Tonle Sap and Mekong rivers.

2. Riverfront Serenity:

The Rivergarden, Kampot: The Rivergarden in Kampot welcomes you to relax by the river. Enjoy a relaxed atmosphere with a cuisine that includes both foreign and Khmer delicacies. This riverfront jewel creates a tranquil setting for a leisurely dinner.

3. The Mekong River Charm:

The Landing Zone, Kratie: Experience the beauty of the Mekong River at The Landing Zone in Kratie. This quaint café serves a variety of Khmer and Western dishes. Enjoy a riverbank dinner while watching the dolphins that inhabit the neighboring seas.

4. Sunset Cruise Dining:

Mango Cruises, Siem Reap: Enjoy a gorgeous cruise and delicious meals on Mango Cruises in Siem Reap. Sail over the gorgeous rivers while enjoying a delicious supper as the sun sets over the horizon. This unique trip combines gastronomic delights with the grandeur of Cambodia's surroundings.

5. Authentic floating restaurants:

Visit the Koh Pdao Floating Restaurant in Kampong Cham for a real riverfront experience. Indulge in traditional Khmer cuisine while surrounded by the tranquil waters of the Mekong River. The floating setting lends an element of authenticity to your eating experience.

Cambodia's culinary scene caters to a wide range of tastes, whether you prefer the historical ambiance of a colonial-era house, the tranquility of riverside dining, or the thrill of sky-high views. Discover the distinct surroundings and flavors of Khmer cuisine for an exceptional dining experience in this interesting country.

8.3 Vegetarian and Dietary Options

Cambodia's culinary landscape caters to a wide range of tastes and dietary preferences. Explore the rich tapestry of flavors that caters to all palates, from vegan delights to vegetarian-friendly restaurants.

Catering to Different Dietary Preferences

1. Different Street Food Options:

Cambodia's vibrant street food scene includes a variety of vegetarian and vegan options. Explore markets and street stalls for dishes like vegetable spring rolls, grilled corn, and fresh fruit smoothies, which are both delicious and nutritious.

2. Market freshness:

For a variety of fresh fruits, vegetables, and plant-based snacks, head to local markets like Psar Chaa in Siem Reap or Psar Thmei in Phnom Penh. Immerse yourself in the lively atmosphere while learning about local ingredients to prepare your own vegetarian meals.

3. Khmer Salad Varieties:

Enjoy the vibrant flavors of Khmer salads, such as the popular green mango salad and pomelo salad. These salads, packed with fresh ingredients, are a refreshing and healthy vegetarian meal option.

4. Rice and Noodle Staple:

Try Cambodian staple dishes with vegetarian twists. These hearty meals, which range from vegetable-studded fried rice to tofu or vegetable stir-fried noodles, highlight Khmer cuisine's versatility.

Vegan and Vegetarian-Friendly Places

1. Vibe Café in Siem Reap:

Plant-Based Paradise: The Vibe Café in Siem Reap is a vegan and vegetarian haven. This cafe caters to those looking for cruelty-free and nutritious plant-based options, with a diverse menu that includes Buddha bowls as well as vegan burgers.

2. Artillery in Phnom Penh:

Creative Vegan Cuisine: ARTillery in Phnom Penh is well-known for its innovative vegan dishes. With a focus on sustainability, the restaurant prepares flavorful plant-based meals such as vegan wraps, nourishing bowls, and dairy-free desserts.

3. Chamkar, Siem Reap:

Khmer Vegetarian Specialties: Chamkar in Siem Reap is a vegetarian restaurant that specializes in Khmer plant-based cuisine. Indulge in dishes like the Amok Chay (vegetarian version of the traditional fish amok) and flavorful curries made with fresh, local ingredients.

4. Friends the Restaurant, Phnom Penh and Siem Reap:

Socially Responsible Dining: Friends the Restaurant, with locations in both Phnom Penh and Siem Reap, not only serves vegetarian and vegan options but also supports a good cause. Run by an NGO, the restaurant offers training and employment opportunities to marginalized youth.

5. Dosa Corner, Phnom Penh:

South Indian Delights: Dosa Corner in Phnom Penh specializes in South Indian cuisine, providing a range of vegetarian and vegan dosas, idlis, and curries. Immerse yourself in the rich and spicy flavors of South India right in the heart of Cambodia's capital.

6. Vegetarian-Friendly Street Markets:

Explore Local Markets: Many local street markets offer a variety of vegetarian and vegan options. Look for stalls serving stir-fried vegetables, tofu skewers, and plant-based noodle dishes. Engage with local vendors to customize your meals according to your dietary preferences.

Whether you're a dedicated vegan or simply looking for vegetarian-friendly options, Cambodia's culinary scene invites you to explore a diverse range of plant-based delights. From vibrant street food to specialized restaurants, savor the flavors of this Southeast Asian gem while adhering to your dietary choices.

8.4 Local Markets

Discover the heart and soul of Cambodian cuisine at its bustling local markets, where the sounds of daily life blend seamlessly with the aromas of fresh produce and exotic spices. Explore these bustling hubs to immerse yourself in Cambodia's culinary culture, sample delicious snacks, and find one-of-a-kind souvenirs to take home.

Exploring Vibrant Markets for Fresh Produce

1. Psar Chaa, Siem Reap:

Market Highlights: Psar Chaa, also known as the Old Market, is a must-visit destination for food enthusiasts. Here, you'll find an eclectic array of fresh fruits, vegetables, herbs, and spices, showcasing the vibrant colors and flavors of Cambodian cuisine.

2. Psar Thmei, Phnom Penh:

Art Deco Marvel: Psar Thmei, or the Central Market, is a Phnom Penh landmark renowned for its stunning art deco architecture. Inside, you'll discover a labyrinth of stalls offering everything from fresh seafood and meat to tropical fruits and fragrant herbs.

3. Psar Leu, Sihanoukville:

Coastal Delights: Psar Leu in Sihanoukville is a bustling market where you can sample an array of fresh seafood straight from the Gulf of Thailand. Explore the stalls filled with colorful fish, prawns, crabs, and shellfish, reflecting the coastal bounty of the region.

4. Psar Nat, Battambang:

Local Flavors: Psar Nat in Battambang is a traditional Khmer market where you can experience the authentic flavors of Cambodia. Browse through stalls offering a diverse range of fresh produce, including exotic fruits, aromatic herbs, and locally grown vegetables.

Snacks and Souvenirs at the Night Market

1. Angkor Night Market, Siem Reap:

Shopping and Dining: The Angkor Night Market in Siem Reap is a bustling hub of activity where you can shop for souvenirs and sample delicious street food. Browse through rows of stalls selling handmade crafts, clothing, and artwork, then indulge in tasty treats like grilled meats, fried noodles, and fresh fruit shakes.

2. Phsar Reatrey, Phnom Penh:

Riverside Charm: Phsar Reatrey, or the Riverside Night Market, in Phnom Penh offers a scenic backdrop for an evening of shopping and dining. Stroll along the Mekong River promenade as you browse through stalls selling local handicrafts, jewelry, and clothing, then savor Khmer delicacies at the food stalls lining the waterfront.

3. Phsar Chas, Kampot:

Rustic Charm: Phsar Chas, or the Old Market, in Kampot exudes a rustic charm that harks back to a bygone era. Explore the narrow alleyways and wooden stalls filled with an assortment of goods, including spices, textiles, and handmade souvenirs. Don't forget to sample the local street food, such as grilled meats and savory snacks.

4. Phsar Kandal, Battambang:

Local Culture: Phsar Kandal in Battambang offers a glimpse into the daily lives of locals as they shop for fresh produce and household items. Wander through the maze of stalls and haggle with vendors for the best deals on fruits, vegetables, and spices. Be sure to try some traditional Cambodian snacks, such as rice cakes and coconut desserts.

Experience the vibrant sights, sounds, and flavors of Cambodia at its bustling local markets. Whether you're in search of fresh produce, unique souvenirs, or delicious street food, these markets offer a glimpse into the rich culinary heritage of the country.

Chapter 9: Festivals and Events

9.1 Cambodian New Year

Experience the vibrant and cheerful celebrations of Khmer New

Year, a traditional holiday that kicks off the Khmer year. This yearly celebration, known as "Chaul Chnam Thmey" in Khmer, is one of Cambodia's most important and highly awaited festivals. Immerse yourself in the bustling atmosphere as the people celebrate the New Year with colorful events and cultural traditions.

Celebrate the Traditional New Year

1. Date and Duration:

The Khmer New Year is traditionally celebrated in mid-April and lasts three days, according to the lunar calendar. The exact dates may change each year, so check the local calendar for the actual time of the celebrations.

2. Water Festival:

One of the highlights of Khmer New Year is the traditional water celebration, known as "Songkran." During this time, people engage in water fights and playful splashing to wash away the sins of the previous year and signify a new beginning for the New Year. The streets are crowded with revelers equipped with water pistols and buckets, creating a festive and refreshing environment.

3. Offering blessings:

Another prominent feature of Khmer New Year is "bathing" Buddha statues and bestowing blessings on monks and elders. Families gather at temples to pour fragrant water on Buddha images as a sign of reverence and cleaning. It is also common to request blessings from monks and receive them in exchange for good luck and prosperity in the next year.

Festivals and Cultural Events

1. Traditional Ceremony:

Throughout Khmer New Year, Cambodians participate in a variety of traditional ceremonies to celebrate ancestors and cultural heritage. These events frequently feature colorful processions, traditional music and dance performances, and religious rituals led by Buddhist monks.

2. Street celebrations:

During Khmer New Year, large cities and towns come alive with busy marketplaces, street vendors offering festive snacks and delicacies, and exciting performances celebrating Khmer culture. Visitors can take part in the celebrations by playing traditional games, consuming local cuisine, and watching live music and dance performances.

3. Community gatherings:

Khmer New Year is a time for families and communities to gather and unite over common traditions and customs. From extravagant feasts to intimate house gatherings, the sense of community pervades every part of the event. Visitors are frequently invited to partake in these social festivals, which provide a unique opportunity to experience Khmer hospitality firsthand.

Plan Your Khmer New Year Experience

1. Accommodation:

Due to the popularity of Khmer New Year, it is best to book accommodations well in advance, particularly in tourist hotspots such as Siem Reap and Phnom Penh. Many hotels and guesthouses provide special specials and packages during the festival, allowing tourists to enjoy the festivities in comfort and style.

2. Respect local customs:

While Khmer New Year is a time for pleasure and celebration, it is critical to uphold local customs and traditions. When visiting temples or participating in religious events, visitors should dress modestly and refrain from engaging in any disrespectful or inappropriate behavior.

3. Keep Hydrated and Protected:

With temperatures rising throughout Khmer New Year, it's critical to stay hydrated and protected from the sun. Carry lots of water, use sunscreen, and seek shade whenever feasible, especially if you're taking part in outdoor events or street festivals.

Khmer New Year provides an intriguing peek into Cambodian culture and traditions, with its vivid festivals and cheerful celebrations. Whether you participate in the water battles, eat wonderful street food, or seek blessings at a temple, this yearly event guarantees a unique experience for people from all over the world.

9.2 Water Festival.

Take a thrilling voyage into the heart of Cambodia's annual Water Festival, which is famous for its stunning boat racing and bustling waterfront activities. Join the locals for an immersive event blending tradition, competitiveness, and social joy.

The Annual Boat Race Extravaganza

1. Significance and tradition:

The Water Festival, also known as "Bon Om Touk," is a time-honored ritual that marks the end of the rainy season and the Tonle Sap River's reversing flow. This three-day event is enjoyed across the country, with boat races acting as the main attraction. The races reflect the Khmer people's strength, solidarity, and persistence.

2. Boat Design and Teams:

Admire the beauty of beautifully adorned longboats, each operated by a committed crew of rowers. These traditional boats feature complex decorations and brilliant colors, frequently symbolizing different provinces and towns. The competition is fierce, and the teams who participate put forth a lot of effort in training and planning.

3. Racecourses and Excitement:

The boat races take place on the Tonle Sap River, and the categories range from small canoes to large dragon boats. The courses are purposefully constructed to test the rowers' skills and endurance, presenting spectators with an exciting show of speed, agility, and collaboration. The atmosphere is electrifying, with cheers and anticipation as the boats rush to the finish line.

Joining Locals in Waterfront Celebrations

1. Riverside Festivities:

As the boat races take place on the river, the riverbanks come alive with colorful festivities. Join the locals in celebrating around the riverfront, which features lively marketplaces, live entertainment, and a plethora of street food booths selling delectable Khmer delicacies and treats. It's a fantastic opportunity to immerse oneself in Cambodia's diverse cultural heritage.

2. Fireworks and illumination:

As the sun sets, prepare for a spectacular display of fireworks to illuminate the night sky. The brilliant hues bounce off the water, creating a stunning spectacle. Many people and visitors congregate along the riverbanks to watch the spectacular fireworks display, adding to the celebratory atmosphere.

3. Concerts and Cultural Performances:

Live music, traditional dance performances, and cultural exhibitions will bring you closer to Cambodian culture. Various stages along the riverfront showcase a variety of performances that highlight the richness and talent of Cambodia's artistic community. From traditional Khmer dance to contemporary music, the Water Festival provides a sensory feast for attendees.

Plan Your Water Festival Experience

1. Accommodation at the Riverside

To completely immerse yourself in the Water Festival experience, consider staying along the river in places such as Phnom Penh or Siem Reap. This gives you a front-row seat to the boat races and quick access to the lively events. Guesthouses, motels, and riverside resorts provide a variety of options to suit varied interests and budgets.

2. How to Navigate Crowds and Transportation

Due to the popularity of the Water Festival, expect heavy crowds around the riverbanks. Plan your transportation carefully, as certain roads may be closed for the festivities. Tuk-tuks, cyclos, and walking are frequently the most expedient ways to navigate congested places.

3. Cultural Sensitivity:

When celebrating, follow local customs and traditions. Dress modestly when visiting temples or attending religious ceremonies. Avoid any impolite or inappropriate behavior at this traditional festival.

The Water Festival offers a unique opportunity to experience

Cambodia's colorful spirit and deep-rooted customs. Whether you're cheering on the boat races, feasting in local foods, or enjoying cultural performances, this yearly festival promises to be a remarkable and engaging experience for travelers looking to get to the heart of Khmer culture.

9.3 Angkor Photography Festival

Embark on a visual trip at the Angkor Photo Festival, an annual event that brings together international and local photographers in the heart of Cambodia's cultural hub. Immerse yourself in the exciting world of visual storytelling, interact with the artistic community, and observe images' capacity to transmit varied narratives.

Showcases International and Local Photography

1. A Celebration of Visual Storytelling:

The Angkor Photo Festival, held yearly in Siem Reap, provides a venue for photographers from across the world to express their visual narratives. This event celebrates storytelling through a lens, capturing experiences, emotions, and viewpoints that cross cultural boundaries. From documentary to high art, the festival demonstrates the diversity and impact of photography as a means of expression.

2. Various Exhibitions and Themes:

Visit a variety of exhibitions exhibiting works by both young and established photographers. The festival covers a wide range of topics, including social challenges, cultural diversity, environmental concerns, and personal stories. Visitors can expect thought-provoking exhibitions that illuminate the human experience while stimulating reflection and conversation.

3. Interactive installation and workshops:

Explore photography on a deeper level with interactive installations and seminars led by renowned photographers. These courses allow participants to learn about various photography techniques, storytelling approaches, and the creative process. Whether you're a novice photographer or a seasoned pro, the Angkor Photo Festival provides an opportunity for learning and collaboration.

Connecting with the Artistic Community

1. Artist Talks & Panel Discussions:

Attend artist talks and panel discussions to gain insight into photographers' ideas. Learn about their creative methods, inspirations, and the tales behind their stunning photos. The festival encourages a sense of community by allowing attendees to contact with artists, ask questions, and engage in conversations that cross language barriers using the universal language of visual storytelling.

2. Networking Opportunities:

Network with other photographers, artists, and industry professionals at various events. Whether you're a photography enthusiast looking for like-minded people or a new photographer trying to establish meaningful contacts, the Angkor Photo Festival offers an ideal setting for networking and collaboration.

3. Cultural exchange and community engagement:

Aside from the installations, the festival promotes cultural interchange by include local perspectives. Collaborations with Cambodian photographers and involvement in the local community enhance the overall experience, presenting a complete picture of Cambodia's cultural tapestry. Attendees can participate in community-focused photographic activities, which build a sense of shared creativity and understanding.

Plan Your Angkor Photo Festival Experience

1. Siem Reap Accommodation Options:

Siem Reap has a variety of hotel alternatives to suit different interests and budgets. From boutique guesthouses to luxury resorts, reserve your stay ahead of time, especially around festival days. Locations near festival venues provide easy access to exhibitions and events.

2. Festival Schedule and Venues:

Plan your visit around the festival schedule. The Angkor Photo Festival normally lasts several days, with exhibitions and events held at various locations across Siem Reap. Familiarize yourself with the sites so you can make the most of your time and explore the variety of services.

3. Ticket Details and Workshops:

Stay up to date on ticket information and any workshops or programs that require pre-registration. Some events may have a limited capacity, so reserving your spot in advance guarantees you don't miss out on unique exhibitions or interactive activities.

4. Cultural Sensitivity:

Respect the festival's local customs and practices. Siem Reap is home to the spectacular Angkor Wat, and visitors are invited to experience the region's cultural history with respect.

The Angkor Photo Festival brings together art, culture, and global viewpoints in a unique way. Immerse yourself in the world of visual storytelling, interact with the artistic community, and embrace the varied narratives presented. You'll leave with a greater respect for photography's ability to link hearts and minds across boundaries.

9.4 Dance and Musical Performances

Experience Cambodia's unique cultural history through engaging dance and music performances. Immerse yourself in the rich tapestry of Khmer arts and traditions, from delicate Apsara dance motions to rhythmic sounds of traditional folk music.

Traditional Apsara Dance and Folk Music

1. Apsara Dance:

The Apsara dance is a traditional Khmer dance form that dates back to the Angkorian era. The Apsara dance, inspired by celestial nymphs seen in ancient temple carvings, uses movement to embody elegance, grace, and narrative. Dancers dressed in ornate costumes and intricate headdresses perform legendary tales and cultural narratives to traditional Khmer music.

2. Folk music:

Traditional Khmer folk music is distinguished by both melodic simplicity and rhythmic complexity. The tro, a form of bamboo xylophone, and the chapey, a long-necked lute, provide charming tunes that capture the essence of rural Cambodia. Folk songs frequently praise themes such as love, nature, and everyday life, representing the Khmer cultural identity.

Where to See Authentic Performances

1. Apsara Dance performances:

Siem Reap, home of the majestic Angkor Wat temple complex, has various opportunities to see Apsara dance performances. Many hotels and restaurants in the neighborhood provide weekly dinner presentations featuring traditional Khmer food and live Apsara dance performances. These performances offer an unforgettable cultural experience in a lovely environment.

2. Cultural shows and theatres:

Apsara dance and traditional folk music performances are often showcased at cultural centers and theaters in major towns such as Phnom Penh and Siem Reap. These venues provide immersive cultural experiences that allow spectators to witness the beauty and talent of Khmer dancers and musicians up close.

3. Traditional villages and temples:

Visit rural villages and old temples to experience true Khmer culture. Local villages frequently organize traditional dance and music performances for festivals and special events, giving tourists a glimpse into everyday Khmer life and traditions. Engaging with local populations promotes cultural interchange and appreciation.

Plan Your Cultural Experience

1. Accommodation Options:

When planning a trip to Cambodia, consider staying in lodgings close to cultural and performing sites. This provides easy access to Apsara dance acts and folk music performances, enhancing your cultural immersion experience.

2. Ticketing and reservations:

Many Apsara dance performances require advanced bookings, particularly during peak tourist seasons. To secure your position, check the schedule and reserve your tickets ahead of time. Some cultural acts may offer dinner packages that include both the performance and a typical Khmer meal.

3. Cultural sensitivity:

When watching traditional dance and music performances, keep in mind their cultural value. Respect the artists and their cultural heritage by adhering to appropriate dress requirements and refraining from disruptive behavior during performances.

4. Supporting local artists:

Show your respect for Khmer arts and culture by supporting local musicians and artists. Consider getting handcrafted goods, musical instruments, or recordings of traditional Khmer music as keepsakes. Your assistance helps us preserve and promote Cambodia's cultural heritage.

Chapter 10: Transportation

10.1 Going to Angkor Wat

Starting your journey to Angkor Wat involves careful planning and evaluation of numerous transportation alternatives. Whether you prefer the convenience of flying or the scenic beauty of bus travel, understanding the logistics will ensure a smooth arrival in Siem Reap, the gateway to the famed temple complex.

Flights, Buses, and Transportation Hubs

1. Flights to Siem Reap: The most effective way to get to Siem Reap, the city nearest to Angkor Wat, is by plane. Siem Reap International Airport (REP) is well connected to major international airports, with direct flights from Bangkok, Singapore, and Kuala Lumpur. Upon arrival, you will find easy transportation to Angkor Wat and your chosen accommodation.

2. **Overland Travel by Bus:** Overland bus travel is a cheap and

scenic choice for those looking for a more adventurous journey. Buses connect major cities in Cambodia and neighboring countries. Phnom Penh, Cambodia's capital, is a popular starting place for bus excursions to Siem Reap. Prepare for a lengthier travel time than flights, but the journey provides glimpses into Cambodia's landscapes and local life.

3. Transportation hubs in Cambodia: Phnom Penh acts as a transportation center, with a variety of routes linking to Siem Reap. Sihanoukville and Battambang are other popular destinations for vacationers touring Cambodia's various regions. Choose your transportation hub based on your preferred itinerary and the destinations you intend to see before or after Angkor Wat.

Tips for Easy Travel to Siem Reap

1. Book Flights and Tickets: Consider reserving your airline or bus tickets ahead of time to get the greatest rates. Online platforms and travel firms offer handy ways to reserve tickets, allowing you to arrange your trip with simplicity. Before booking, make sure you are aware of any travel limitations or visa requirements.

2. Airport Transfers and Taxi: To ensure a smooth transition from Siem Reap International Airport to your accommodation, make arrangements for airport transfers or taxis ahead of time. Many hotels provide shuttle services, or you can order a taxi from the airport. To ensure trustworthiness, agree on the fare ahead of time and choose registered taxi services.

3. Local transportation in Siem Reap: Explore Siem Reap and its surroundings with a variety of transportation choices. Tuk-tuks are a popular and economical mode of transportation in Cambodia, offering a one-of-a-kind experience. Bicycle rentals and motorcycle taxis are also available for those who want to explore independently.

4. Hire a Private Driver: Consider hiring a private driver to transport you to Angkor Wat and other local sights. Private drivers can modify the schedule to your tastes and provide information about local culture and history.

5. Time Management: - Plan your arrival in Siem Reap strategically, taking into account the optimum times to visit Angkor Wat. The early morning and late afternoon provide spectacular sights and cooler temps. This planning ensures that you get the most out of your time exploring the temples.

6. Staying Informed: - Be aware of any travel advisories, weather conditions, or road closures that may impact your route. Check credible sources for information on a regular basis, and have backup plans in place in case your trip itinerary changes unexpectedly.

By carefully picking your mode of transportation, planning ahead, and remaining informed, you may ensure a smooth trip to Siem Reap and a pleasurable exploration of Angkor Wat. Whether you like the comfort of air travel or the picturesque beauty of overland busses, your transportation experience becomes an important part of your vacation in this captivating location.

10.2 Getting Around Angkor Archaeological Park.

To fully explore the enormous and fascinating Angkor Archaeological Park, you'll need reliable transportation. Understanding the different options, ranging from traditional tuk-tuks to guided excursions, provides a smooth and comfortable journey across the park's breathtaking surroundings.

Tuk-Tuks, Bicycles, and Guided Tours

1. Tuk-tuks: The classic Cambodian tuk-tuk is a popular and practical form of transportation at Angkor Archaeological Park. Tuk-tuks provide an open-air environment in which you may appreciate the surroundings while commuting between temples. They are widely accessible around the park's entrances and main temples. Negotiate fares prior to your trip, and consider hiring a tuk-tuk driver for the day to see numerous temples at your leisure.

2. Bicycles: - Renting a bicycle is an eco-friendly option to see Angkor Wat and its surroundings. Several rental businesses near the park's gates sell bicycles, and the flat topography makes cycling between temples fun. Bring water, sunscreen, and start your tour early to escape the midday heat.

3. Guided tours: A competent guide on a tour of Angkor Wat and the neighboring temples enriches your experience by offering historical and cultural context. Many guides provide solo or group trips, personalizing the schedule to your needs. Whether you're interested in the architectural features of Angkor Wat or the cryptic sculptures of Ta Prohm, a guided tour will give you a better grasp of the site's significance.

Efficient Transportation in the Park

To visit Angkor Wat, obtain a temple pass from the official ticketing center. Passes are offered for one, three, or seven days, giving users greater flexibility when touring the park. Keep your pass with you at all times, as it will be examined upon entry into each temple.

2. Park Shuttles: – The Angkor Park shuttle system is a cost-effective and handy way to travel between temples. These shuttle buses follow predefined itineraries, stopping at significant temples and other areas of interest. The shuttles offer a comfortable and effective mode of transportation, especially for those who visit numerous temples in a single day.

3. Personal Vehicles:- Some visitors choose to explore Angkor Wat in their own vehicles, such as cars or motorcycles. While this provides flexibility in terms of timetable and route, it is vital to be cautious of parking laws.

Restrictions apply within the park. Make sure your vehicle is appropriate for the terrain, and consider hiring a local driver if you don't want to manage the roads alone.

4. Foot Exploration: - Walking through temple complexes highlights detailed features and immerses you in the ancient ambiance. Walking may not be practical for crossing great distances between temples, but it is an excellent way to appreciate the unique beauty of each location.

5. Sunrise and Sunset Options: - Plan your transportation to Angkor Wat to experience the spectacular sunrise and sunset. Tuk-tuks frequently provide morning packages, allowing you to arrive at the main temple well before daybreak. For sunset, try visiting the Terrace of the Elephants or Phnom Bakheng, both of which are accessible by various modes of transportation.

6. Accessibility Considerations: - Angkor Wat aims to improve accessibility for all visitors. While not all temples are wheelchair accessible, several walkways and entrances have been modified to better accommodate persons with mobility issues. Check in advance for accessibility information and inquire about available services.

Navigating Angkor Archaeological Park is a delightful trip, with transportation alternatives to suit a variety of preferences and interests. Whether you prefer the charm of a tuk-tuk, the freedom of a bicycle, or the insights provided by a guided tour, the park's efficient movement allows you to fully immerse yourself in the glories of Angkor Wat and its magnificent temples.

10.3 Day Tours & Excursions

Beyond the mesmerizing limits of Angkor Archaeological Park, the neighboring districts provide a plethora of day trip options to compliment your Angkor Wat experience. Exploring these nearby treasures allows you to delve further into Cambodia's rich cultural tapestry. Here are some suggested day trip itineraries to complement your Siem Reap adventure.

Exploring the Surrounding Areas

1. Banteay Srei and Kbal Spean: – Before driving to Kbal Spean, spend the day seeing Banteay Srei, which is famous for its exquisite pink sandstone sculptures. Kbal Spean, also known as the

River of a Thousand Lingas, has ancient engravings along its riverbed. The excursion offers insight into Cambodia's artistic and spiritual legacy.

2. Roluos Group Temples: Visit Preah Ko, Bakong, and Lolei temples. These temples precede Angkor Wat and provide insight into the early Khmer architectural traditions. A day spent seeing Roluos provides historical context for the later magnificence of Angkor Wat.

3. Tonle Sap Lake and Floating Villages: Discover Tonle Sap Lake, Southeast Asia's largest freshwater lake, and its unique ecosystem. Day tours to the lake frequently include visits to floating communities, where you can see everyday life on the water. Engage with local residents to learn about the challenges and resilience of these lakeside settlements.

4. Kulen Mountain National Park: Explore the mystical Kulen Mountain, a UNESCO World Heritage site. Kulen Mountain, which includes the "River of a Thousand Lingas" and the reclining Buddha at Preah Ang Thom, combines natural beauty with historical significance. Cool off in the soothing waters of Kulen's waterfalls for a revitalizing experience.

Recommended Day Trip Itineraries

1. Angkor Thom Circuit: – Begin your day by exploring the majesty of Angkor Thom, including Bayon Temple with its enigmatic smiling faces and the Terrace of the Elephants. Continue to Baphuon and the Royal Enclosure, taking in the historical significance of this old city.

2. Temples for Small Circuits: Spend a day exploring the Small Circuit, beginning with the magnificent Angkor Wat at sunrise. Explore Ta Prohm, which is noted for its intertwined tree roots, as well as Banteay Kdei and Srah Srang. This trip combines architectural marvels with calm settings.

3. Rural Countryside Adventure: - Extend your exploration beyond temples to the countryside. Explore the colorful local culture, meet with farmers, and cycle through breathtaking landscapes. This full day excursion offers a different perspective outside of the religious complexes.

4. Grand Circuit Expedition:- Visit temples including Preah Khan, Neak Pean, and East Mebon. This less-crowded approach offers for a more thoughtful observation of the many temple structures and architectural styles.

5. Kulen Waterfall Discovery: Spend the day exploring Kulen Mountain National Park's natural wonders. Explore the cascading waterfalls and River of a Thousand Lingas. This journey mixes cultural and ecological components, resulting in a complete experience.

Practical Tips for Day Trips

1. Transportation: - Plan reliable transportation for day trips, including private drivers, guided tours, and rental vehicles. Confirm the itinerary with your preferred method of transportation to guarantee a seamless journey.

2. Local Guides: - Use local guides to gain a deeper understanding of the sites you visit. Their insights on history, culture, and local stories enrich your exploration.

3. Meals and Refreshments: - Bring snacks and remain hydrated during your day trips. While certain regions may offer local restaurants, having necessities can keep you energized during your trip.

4. Respectful Exploration: - Follow ethical tourist practices while respecting local communities and historical sites. Reduce your environmental footprint by leaving each destination as you found it.

Day tours from Siem Reap allow you to explore Cambodia's history and culture beyond the iconic Angkor Wat. Tailor your explorations to your interests, whether historic temples, rural landscapes, or natural wonders, to ensure a well-rounded and rewarding travel experience.

Chapter 11: Hidden Gems

11.1 Lesser-Known Temples.

As you explore the ancient wonders of Angkor, you'll be enthralled by the grandeur of well-known temples such as Angkor Wat, Bayon, and Ta Prohm. However, the temple-dotted landscape hides a plethora of lesser-known gems, offering an intimate and tranquil getaway from the bustling crowds. Explore the secret temples that add a mysterious touch to your Angkor adventure.

Off-Beaten-Path Temple Exploration

1. Banteay Samré: – Banteay Samré, located in the eastern portion of Angkor, is a hidden jewel that resembles Angkor Wat's architectural style but on a smaller scale. The beautiful sculptures and well-preserved structures provide a peaceful contrast to the more busy temples.

2. Beng Mealea: For a genuine off-the-beaten-path excursion, head to Beng Mealea, which is just 40 kilometers from Siem Reap. This huge temple, mostly unrestored and surrounded by nature, offers an Indiana Jones-like experience. Explore the labyrinthine corridors and admire the exquisite stone carvings.

3. Preah Khan from Kompong Svay: The isolated Preah Khan of Kompong Svay, which requires a longer trek, is a massive temple complex surrounded by Cambodian farmland. This hidden gem provides a tranquil ambiance, allowing you to explore at your own speed without the usual tourist hordes.

4. Banteay Thom: - Located near the well-known Ta Prohm, Banteay Thom is often overlooked. This temple, with its crumbling towers and lovely gardens, encourages you to explore history in relative seclusion.

5. Koh Ker: - Known for its towering pyramid, Prasat Thom, Koh Ker exemplifies the Khmer Empire's architectural brilliance. The voyage to Koh Ker offers not only historical lessons, but also the opportunity to enjoy the calm of Cambodia's countryside.

Serenity Away from Crowds

1. Ascend Phnom Bok for a panoramic perspective of Angkor Wat, away from crowds. This hilltop temple provides a tranquil setting and a stunning view of the enormous Angkor complex.

2. Chau Say Tevoda: – Chau Say Tevoda, located on the east side of Angkor Thom, may be overshadowed by its more famous neighbors, but its beautiful sculptures and tranquil environment make it an ideal refuge.

3. Ta Nei: - Find peace at Ta Nei, a modest shrine surrounded by vegetation. The lack of visitors allows for a more intimate experience in which you can absorb the ancient essence of the location.

4. Prasat Kravan: – Prasat Kravan, located just outside the bustling city of Angkor Thom, is a simple sanctuary with distinctive brick decorations. Its relative obscurity ensures a peaceful stay while allowing you to connect with the temple's spiritual core.

5) Preah Pithu Group: The Preah Pithu Group, which consists of a cluster of modest temples, is often neglected. This secret ensemble offers a tranquil environment for reflection amidst the ancient ruins.

Practical Tips for Exploring Hidden Temples

1. Local Guides: - Use local guides who are conversant with lesser-known temples. Their views might help you appreciate the historical and cultural significance of these hidden gems.

2. Timing is Key: - Visit these temples at off-peak hours or at sunrise or sunset. This guarantees a more peaceful experience and allows you to take in the sights uninterrupted.

3. considerate Exploration: - As with all Angkor temples, tourists should be considerate. Follow the rules, stay on specified walkways, and avoid touching fragile carvings to protect these hidden treasures for future generations.

4. Transportation: - Plan reliable transportation, especially for hidden temples in distant places. Plan your mode of transportation, whether it's a tuk-tuk, bicycle, or guided tour, to ensure a smooth journey.

Unlock the secrets of Angkor by deviating from the well-trodden paths. These hidden temples not only provide historical marvels, but also the tranquillity sought by those seeking a deeper connection with Cambodia's ancient history.

11.2 Local Artisans and Workshops

Beyond the ancient temples, Angkor provides a vivid tapestry of contemporary Cambodian culture via its local artists and workshops. Exploring true Cambodian workmanship offers a unique opportunity to engage with the region's living legacy. Discover the hands and hearts that create traditional arts and crafts while actively helping local craftsmen in maintaining their cultural heritage.

Discovering Authentic Cambodian Craftsmanship

1. Artisans of Angkor: Artisans Angkor is a social company that supports ancient Khmer arts and a shining example of Cambodian workmanship. This studio and boutique in Siem Reap showcases a wide range of crafts, including silk weaving, stone carving, lacquerware, and silver plating. Engage with artists, watch their careful methods, and purchase wonderful handmade keepsakes straight from the source.

2. Angkor Handicraft Association: - Explore the cooperative of local craftspeople outside of tourist-heavy regions. Traditional methods like as silk painting, wood carving, and silverwork are carefully conserved here. The intimate atmosphere enables one-on-one discussions with artists eager to give insights into their profession.

3. Phare and the Cambodian Circus: While not a typical workshop, Phare, The Cambodian Circus, is a fascinating showcase of contemporary Cambodian art. This social venture helps Cambodian teenagers find work and pursue their artistic interests. Attend a performance to see a blend of acrobatics, theater, and Cambodian storytelling while supporting the country's emerging performing arts community.

4. Cambodia Landmine Museum and Relief Center: Beyond traditional crafts, the Cambodia Landmine Museum and Relief Center near Siem Reap offers a unique perspective on socially conscious craftsmanship. This museum displays sculptures made from decommissioned landmines and unexploded ordnance, bringing art and awareness to the impact of fighting in Cambodia.

5. Pottery Workshops on Koh Ker: Visit Koh Ker, an archaeological site with buried temples, and find local pottery workshops. Engage with craftsmen as they shape clay into exquisite forms, demonstrating the age-old heritage of Cambodian pottery. Participate in a hands-on pottery lesson and make your own keepsake.

Supporting Local Artisans

1. Make Informed Purchases: - Choose souvenirs made by local craftsmen. Make wise selections that help to preserve traditional craftsmanship.

2. personalized Commissions: - Create personal connections with craftspeople by commissioning personalized creations. This not only creates a one-of-a-kind remembrance, but it also directly benefits the artisan's livelihood.

3. Attend Workshops: - Many workshops include hands-on experiences, allowing visitors to practice traditional crafts. Attend a workshop to learn more about the skills required and to help keep these artistic traditions alive.

4. Share your experiences with local artisans on social media. Spreading the word about these underground workshops helps to raise the artists' awareness and encourages others to support their efforts.

5. Sustainable activities:- Attend workshops that stress sustainable and ethical activities. Supporting craftspeople who utilize sustainable materials and fair labor methods benefits both the environment and the local community.

Practical Tips for Discovering Local Artisans

1. Local Guides: - Use local guides to navigate various seminars. Their insights can help you find hidden gems and have an authentic experience.

2. Transportation: - Plan for reliable transportation, especially when visiting workshops outside of popular tourist regions. Tuk-tuks, bicycles, and guided tours can let you explore seamlessly.

3. Approach craftspeople with respect and interest. Many people want to share their skill, but they should be cautious of their work hours and avoid upsetting their creative processes.

4. Flexible Itinerary: - Allow time to immerse yourself in workshops. Serendipitous discoveries frequently result in the most gratifying experiences.

Discover Cambodia's living cultures by immersing yourself in the world of local craftspeople. From traditional crafts to contemporary expressions, each workshop has its own narrative of resilience, inventiveness, and cultural pride. By actively engaging and supporting these craftspeople, you help to preserve Cambodia's unique cultural history.

11.3 Nature Trails and Birdwatching

While Angkor Wat is known for its ancient temples, the surrounding natural surroundings provide a retreat for nature lovers seeking peace away from the crowded historical attractions. Take nature trails through lush foliage to discover the region's rich biodiversity. Furthermore, bird-watching areas offer the possibility to see a variety of avian species, giving a unique dimension to your Angkor adventure.

Explore the Natural Beauty Surrounding Angkor Wat

1. Angkor Thom's Terrace of the Leper King:** Begin your nature exploration at the Angkor Thom Complex. The Terrace of the Leper King, embellished with beautiful carvings, is surrounded by lush vegetation. Nature pathways close to this terrace allow tranquil treks through tall trees that provide shade and serenity.

2. Angkor Silk Farm Nature Trail: - For an immersive experience, visit the Angkor Silk Farm. Aside from learning about silk production, the farm offers natural walks that run through mulberry farms and gardens. This tranquil refuge allows you to enjoy the local flora and fauna.

3. Phnom Kulen National Park: Explore Phnom Kulen National Park, located beyond the main Angkor complex and noted for its waterfalls and religious significance. Nature pathways wind through deep woodlands, culminating in the breathtaking Kulen Waterfall. Enjoy a pleasant swim in the natural pools created by the flowing water.

4. Kbal Spean: - Kbal Spean, also known as the "River of a Thousand Lingas," is a religious location with beautifully carved riverbed sculptures that line the shallow waters. The hike to Kbal Spean follows a moderate nature walk, allowing you to see the sculptures and the surrounding countryside.

5) Beng Mealea: While Beng Mealea is an outstanding temple in and of itself, getting there requires a hike through the jungle. The thick vegetation surrounding the temple provides an exciting atmosphere, providing the impression of seeking a hidden treasure.

Bird-Watching Hotspots

1. Angkor Thom's South Gate Moat: The moat around Angkor Thom's South Gate is a refuge for bird watchers. Egrets, herons, and other waterfowl can frequently be seen in and around the moat, providing a tranquil bird-watching experience against the backdrop of old buildings.

2. Prek Toal Bird Sanctuary: – Prek Toal Bird Sanctuary, located near Tonle Sap Lake, is a great place to go bird watching. The sanctuary is home to a large number of bird species, including the endangered spot-billed pelican and the greater adjutant. Boat cruises are provided for a close-up look at these gorgeous birds.

3. Angkor Centre for Conservation of Biodiversity (ACCB): -
Learn about Cambodian wildlife at the ACCB, which focuses on
rescuing and rehabilitating native animals. While not a classic bird-
watching location, the facility provides information about local
conservation initiatives, and some rescued birds can be seen during
instructional tours.

4. Tonle Sap Biosphere Reserve: The Tonle Sap Biosphere
Reserve, which includes the Tonle Sap Lake and its surrounds, is
an excellent spot for bird watching. Migratory birds migrate to the
area, and the different habitats provide opportunities to see both
permanent and visiting birds.

5) Angkor Wat Temple Complex: Even within the Angkor Wat
temple complex, keep a watch out for different bird species. The
spacious grounds and surrounding foliage attract a variety of
species, including colorful kingfishers and the majestic Brahminy
kite.

Practical Tips for Nature Trails and Birdwatching

1. Binoculars/Field Guides: Bring binoculars and field guides to improve your bird-watching experience. Local guides may also provide information about the avian species you encounter.

2. Comfortable Footwear: - For a safe and enjoyable walk on nature trails, wear comfortable and durable footwear.

3. Guided Tours: - Hire local guides who are knowledgeable about the vegetation, animals, and bird species. They can improve your comprehension of the natural world.

4. Conservation Awareness: - Keep a respectful distance from wildlife and minimize harm on their habitats. Learn about conservation rules so that you can help protect these natural habitats.

5. Weather Considerations: - Be cautious during rainy season as trails may become slippery. Plan your nature expeditions accordingly.

Explore the hidden natural gems surrounding Angkor Wat and embark on nature walks to discover the beauty beyond the old temples. Whether you're meandering through tranquil landscapes or seeing abundant birds, these experiences provide a welcome counterpoint to the historical wonders, making your Angkor adventure really diverse.

Chapter 12: Wellness and Relaxation

12.1 Spa Retreats.

Spa resorts nestled in the center of Siem Reap, a city rich in history and culture, provide an oasis of leisure amidst the ancient wonders of Angkor Wat. Enjoy rejuvenating spa experiences that elegantly integrate ancient Khmer techniques with current health practices. Here are some spa retreat options to ensure that your trip to Siem Reap is more than just a temple tour, but also a complete wellness retreat.

Revitalizing Spa Experiences in Siem Reap

1. Navutu Dreams Resort & Wellness Retreat: Navutu Dreams, set amidst lovely landscapes, provides a full healing experience. The "Spa & Wellness Sanctuary" here offers a variety of services, including traditional Khmer massages and detoxifying scrubs. The resort's quiet atmosphere contributes to general relaxation, and wellness programs are adapted to individual needs.

2. Bodia Spa: - Bodia Spa offers a rejuvenating experience using natural, locally derived ingredients. The spa offers traditional Khmer massages, aromatherapy, and holistic therapies. Bodia Spa has many locations in Siem Reap, including one along Pub Street, making it easily accessible to those touring the city.

3. Frangipani Spa: Frangipani Spa, nestled in a tropical garden, provides a peaceful respite from the hustle and bustle of city life. The spa specializes in traditional Khmer treatments and massages utilizing locally sourced herbs and oils. The tranquil atmosphere and professional therapists provide a delightful experience from the moment you walk in.

4. Sokkhak Spa: Located near Angkor Wat, Sokkhak Spa offers Khmer-inspired therapies to relax and rejuvenate clients. The spa's use of natural products and professional therapists produces a relaxing ambiance. The "Sokkhak Spa Experience" blends various therapies into a full health journey.

5. Shinta Mani Spa: - Shinta Mani, a luxury resort dedicated to responsible tourism, provides a spa experience that mixes enjoyment and a feeling of purpose. The spa program includes a variety of massages and therapies. The "Bamboo Massage" is an unusual service in which therapists utilize warmed bamboo sticks to knead and roll out tension.

Wellness and Relaxation Recommendations

1. Yoga in Nature:- Spa getaways like Navutu Dreams provide yoga as part of their wellness programs. Engage in rejuvenating yoga classes in the natural setting, fostering a sense of calm and balance.

2. Meditation lessons: - Some spa getaways offer meditation lessons to help you center yourself and practice mindfulness. Connect with professional meditation tutors who will introduce you to Khmer meditation techniques.

3. Healthy Cuisine: - Enhance your spa visit with nutritious meals. Choose spa getaways that serve nutritious cuisine utilizing locally sourced, organic ingredients. Navutu Dreams, for example, blends wellness and a gastronomic trip, serving nutritious and tasty meals.

4. Hot Stone massages:- Enhance your spa experience with hot stone massages that soothe and relax muscles. Many spa getaways, including Bodia Spa, use this approach in their massage services.

5. Couples Retreats: When traveling with a companion, look into spa getaways that include couples' treatments. Share the refreshing experience with your lover, making lasting memories in the tranquil setting of Siem Reap's spa retreats.

Practical Considerations:

1. Make advance reservations for spa retreats in Siem Reap, particularly during peak tourist seasons. Make prior bookings to assure your favorite treatment times and a smooth spa experience.

2. Transportation: - Check if the spa retreat offers transportation services. Some resorts provide complimentary shuttles, making it easier to get to and from the spa.

3. Wellness Packages: Explore spa getaways' wellness packages. These packages frequently mix spa treatments with additional activities, resulting in a holistic well-being experience.

4. Embrace local culture by selecting spa getaways that incorporate traditional Khmer aspects into their treatments. This cultural immersion offers a distinctive element to your healing journey.

5. Cost considerations: While spa vacations provide a variety of packages, consider your budget when choosing services. Some spas may offer promotional packages or seasonal discounts, allowing guests to enjoy premium services at a lower cost.

Experience wellness and relaxation in Siem Reap, where spa getaways perfectly mix traditional Khmer traditions with modern holistic treatments. Amidst the wonders of Angkor Wat, these havens of peace provide a revitalizing vacation, guaranteeing that your visit to Cambodia is not just a historical investigation but also a harmonious retreat for the body and soul.

12.2 Yoga & Meditation

Discovering tranquility among the ancient temples of Angkor Wat is about more than just examining the rich history; it is also about achieving inner harmony. Siem Reap's spiritual ambiance makes it ideal for yoga and meditation. Embrace the calm of this hallowed place with yoga courses and meditation retreats that will connect you with Cambodia's cultural and spiritual core.

Finding Serenity Among Ancient Temples.

1. Prana Yoga & Dance Studio: Located in the heart of Siem Reap, Prana Yoga & Dance Studio provides a peaceful retreat. Join yoga courses that cater to all skill levels, from beginning to experienced practitioner. The studio's unusual location, surrounded by rich nature, creates a tranquil environment for self-discovery.

2. Peace Café: Located near the Siem Reap River, Peace Café promotes healthy living and cultural immersion. The cafe offers daily yoga courses ranging from Hatha to Vinyasa, giving a diverse experience for attendees. After a rejuvenating session, discover the cafe's vegetarian menu, emphasizing a holistic approach to wellness.

3. Navutu Dreams Resort & Wellness Retreat: In addition to spa services, Navutu Dreams is a popular yoga destination. The resort's dedicated yoga pavilion conducts daily lessons, and qualified instructors lead practitioners through a variety of yoga methods. Immerse yourself in the practice from sunrise to sunset, surrounded by the resort's magnificent grounds.

4. Angkor Zen Garden Retreat Center:

For a more immersive experience, visit the Angkor Zen Gardens Retreat Centre. This institution, set in a tropical landscape, provides meditation and yoga retreats. Practice silent meditation as well as everyday yoga. The retreat's holistic approach promotes self-reflection and mindfulness.

5. Green Leaf Boutique Hotel & Luxury Retreat Centre: Enjoy luxury and spiritual wellness with yoga lessons in a tranquil garden setting. The hotel's professional instructors lead participants through Hatha and Ashtanga yoga practices. Join a morning or evening session to align your body and mind.

Yoga Classes and Meditation Retreats

1. Shanti Mani Wild: Located in a private nature sanctuary, Shanti Mani Wild offers eco-luxury and wellness. Join their guided meditation sessions, where the sounds of the surrounding nature add to the experience. The retreat's commitment to conservation complements the introspective character of meditation.

2. Wat Preah Prom Rath Meditation Center: Experience Cambodian spirituality here. Located in Siem Reap, this meditation facility welcomes tourists for guided meditation sessions. Connect with the local community and practice meditation in a cultural setting.

3. Visit Vagabond Temple, a holistic treatment retreat near Siem Reap, to experience a transforming journey. This center offers yoga and meditation retreats and fosters a supportive environment for self-discovery. Engage in silent meditation, yoga nidra, and other techniques to strengthen your spiritual connection.

4. The Living Room Café & Guesthouse near Pub Street offers daily yoga classes on its rooftop patio. With a view of the city, these programs cater to a variety of skill levels, making it an accessible alternative for those looking for wellness while seeing Siem Reap.

5) Phare, the Cambodian Circus:

Phare, the Cambodian Circus, provides a unique blend of

entertainment and mindfulness. Before the evening performances, the group offers circus skills training that incorporate mindfulness exercises. Practice juggling and acrobatics while focusing on the meditative components of these art forms.

Practical considerations

1. Class Schedule:

Check the timetables for yoga courses and meditation retreats in advance. Different venues may offer classes at different times, allowing you to organize your visit to Angkor Wat and other attractions accordingly.

2. Accommodation Packages: Some hotels, including Navutu Dreams and Green Leaf Boutique Hotel, may provide packages that include lodging and wellness activities. Consider these alternatives for a seamless and immersive experience.

3. Choose workshops and retreats based on your ability level, whether you're a beginner or seasoned practitioner. Many locations accommodate a diverse spectrum of attendees, ensuring inclusion.

4. Local Cultural aspects: Select yoga and meditation experiences with local cultural aspects. This increases the authenticity of your practice and provides insight into Cambodian traditions.

5. Respectful Attire: When attending yoga lessons in Cambodia, it's important to dress appropriately for the culture. Comfortable and modest clothes is often appropriate for these activities.

As you tour the temples of Angkor Wat, take time for introspection and rejuvenation with yoga and meditation. Siem Reap's spiritual atmosphere, combined with these wellness options, enables you to delve deeper into the cultural and personal aspects of your journey. Find calm among Cambodia's breathtaking scenery by embracing a balance of traditional traditions and modern mindfulness.

Chapter 13: Nightlife and Entertainment

13.1 Bars and rooftop lounges

When the sun sets over the magnificent backdrop of Angkor Wat, Siem Reap comes alive with a thriving nightlife. The city provides a broad choice of entertainment alternatives, from vibrant bars to calm rooftop lounges, guaranteeing that every tourist can unwind and make unforgettable experiences.

Viewing the Night Sky with a Drink in Hand

1. Pub Street: - Pub Street is the hub of Siem Reap's nightlife. It's the go-to spot for those looking for lively atmospheres and diverse drink options, as it's lined with bars and pubs. The street is noted for its high energy, lively music, and bustling crowds, making it an excellent choice for a night out with friends.

2. Miss Wong Cocktail Bar: Enter the world of Miss Wong Cocktail Bar, a cozy and sophisticated establishment inspired by 1920s Shanghai. This bar, known for its innovative cocktails, provides a pleasant respite from the bustling atmosphere of Pub Street. Enjoy trademark cocktails in a classy setting that takes you to another age.

3. Asana Old Wooden House Bar: Asana Old Wooden House Bar, a one-of-a-kind bar located in a traditional Khmer wooden house, exudes rustic beauty. This bar has a laid-back atmosphere, ideal for people looking for a relaxing evening. Enjoy handcrafted cocktails and local breweries while surrounded by antique décor.

4. Temple Bar: - Temple Bar, with its open-air layout and brilliant lights, creates a dynamic atmosphere for a night of celebration. Dance under the stars to a blend of foreign and Cambodian music. The bar's lively atmosphere makes it popular with both residents and tourists.

5. The Rooftop Lounge at Phum Baitang: For a more sophisticated experience, visit the Rooftop Lounge at Phum Baitang. This luxury resort lounge provides sweeping views of the surrounding landscape. Savor freshly made cocktails while taking in the calm of the verdant surroundings beneath the night sky.

Popular Nightlife Spots

1. What is Angkor? Bar: - Angkor What? Bar is known as one of Siem Reap's original and most renowned bars. This bar is known for its vivid graffiti-covered walls and exudes youthful energy. Join the party for vibrant music, dancing, and a wide selection of drinks.

2. Sombai Liqueur Workshop: Sombai Liqueur Workshop offers a unique and immersive experience. This facility blends entertainment and hands-on activities. Join a workshop to make your own Cambodian liqueur, bringing a personal touch to your nightlife experience.

3. The Warehouse: The Warehouse distinguishes out for its industrial-chic decor and extensive beverage offerings. This venue frequently hosts live music performances and DJ sets, resulting in a lively atmosphere. Enjoy a variety of cocktails, specialty beers, and spirits while taking in the lively atmosphere.

4. Mezze: - Mezze provides a refined setting for visitors looking for a fusion of Middle Eastern and Mediterranean flavors. This elegant lounge not only provides delicious food but also has an amazing cocktail list. It's the perfect pick for a more relaxed evening with a hint of sophistication.

5. Le Malraux:– Le Malraux caters to art and music fans. This facility frequently hosts live bands and art exhibitions, establishing a cultural hub in Siem Reap's nightlife scene. Enjoy a variety of drinks while seeing the local art shown here.

Practical Considerations:

1. Operating Hours: - Many pubs in Siem Reap, particularly on Pub Street, stay open into the early morning. To get the most out of your night out, make sure to check the venue's exact operating hours.

2. Happy Hours and Special Offers: Take advantage of the happy hours and specials that many restaurants provide at specified times. This is a great way to enjoy your favorite drinks for a lower cost.

3. Transportation Options: - Have a dependable plan for returning to your lodging after a night of entertainment. Tuk-tuks and cabs are widely available, and many venues may help arrange transportation if necessary.

4. Dress Code:– While Siem Reap's nightlife scene is largely informal, some locations may need a slightly more dressy attire. Check ahead of time to be sure you're dressed suitably for the occasion.

5. Local insights: Ask locals for recommendations. They frequently have insider information on hidden gems and lesser-known destinations that may suit your tastes.

As you explore Siem Reap's nightlife, you'll discover a great balance of high-energy venues and intimate settings, each providing a distinct experience. Whether you're dancing under the moonlight, drinking cocktails in a chic lounge, or constructing

The city's nightlife will make your evenings as unforgettable as your daytime experiences in the beautiful country of Angkor Wat.

13.2 Cultural Performances.

In the picturesque city of Siem Reap, the nightlife goes beyond bars and lounges, providing a cultural spectacle that captures the soul of Cambodia. Immerse yourself in the region's rich legacy with stunning evening Apsara dance displays and traditional performances that weave an amazing tapestry of entertainment under the night sky.

Evening Apsara Dance Shows and Traditional Performances

1. Phare, the Cambodian Circus: Located near the city center, Phare, the Cambodian Circus offers a breathtaking performance of acrobatics, theater, and contemporary circus arts. Each performance presents a unique story, generally based on Cambodian history and culture. The brilliant artists, many of whom are graduates of the Phare Ponleu Selpak NGO school, put on a dramatic and emotionally packed performance.

2. Apsara Theatre at Angkor Village Resort: For a real Apsara dancing experience, the Apsara Theatre at Angkor Village Resort is highly recommended. Set in verdant gardens, this traditional performance features the graceful Apsara dance, an ancient Cambodian dance genre. The beautiful motions, exquisite costumes, and live music take you to another age.

3. Rosana Broadway Cabaret Show: Enjoy a spectacular cabaret performance with stunning costumes, dancing, and live music. This dynamic play combines contemporary and traditional elements, delivering an enjoyable evening for guests looking for a diversified cultural presentation.

4. Por Cuisine Apsara Dance Theatre.

Por Cuisine Apsara Dance Theatre provides an intimate environment for an Apsara dance performance, followed by a delicious Khmer supper. The combination of traditional cuisine and exquisite dance gives an unforgettable cultural experience in a warm and welcoming setting.

Nightly Entertainment Recommendations

1. Madame Butterfly is a sophisticated lounge that combines Khmer culture and modern entertainment. Enjoy live music performances that range from traditional Cambodian songs to modern favorites. The classy ambiance and extensive music selection make it ideal for a quiet evening.

2. The Village Café is known for its dedication to maintaining Cambodian culture. Aside from serving wonderful Khmer cuisine, this establishment frequently organizes traditional dance

performances. Enjoy the delicacies of Cambodia while being serenaded by the fascinating rhythms of traditional dance.

3. Koulen II Restaurant: This restaurant offers a cultural experience with wonderful Khmer cuisine and nightly Apsara dance shows. This restaurant provides a great blend of gastronomic delights and traditional entertainment, resulting in an all-around cultural experience.

4. Siem Reap Pub Crawl: Explore Siem Reap's nightlife while combining cultural experiences and socializing on this unique tour. The crawl frequently includes stops at live music venues, ensuring an exciting and diverse entertainment experience.

5. Theam's House: Theam's House exemplifies Cambodian creativity. This facility, established by renowned Cambodian artist Lim Muy Theam, not only displays his work but also offers occasional cultural performances. It's a great spot to explore local art and live music.

Practical considerations

1. Cultural performances, particularly in intimate settings, may require reservations. It is recommended that you contact the venue and reserve your space ahead of time, especially during peak

tourist seasons.

2. Show Timings: Venues have various show times and may only provide performances on selected days. Plan your evening properly to avoid missing the cultural performances you want to see.

3. Ticket pricing: Ticket pricing for cultural performances may vary. Some venues include the cost of the entertainment in their dining packages, while others may demand an additional ticket purchase. When making a reservation, make sure to inquire about pricing.

4. Transportation: Confirm the venue's transportation alternatives, especially if it's located outside the city center. This assures a smooth journey to and from the cultural performance.

5. clothes: While Siem Reap is typically informal, some cultural sites may prefer more traditional clothes. Confirm the dress code with the venue to ensure that you are properly dressed for the occasion.

Embark on a cultural journey through the elegance of Apsara dance, the dynamic narrative of the Cambodian Circus, and the colorful energy of traditional performances. Siem Reap's nightlife deviates from the norm, providing a tapestry of cultural encounters to enhance your tour through Cambodia's heart.

Chapter 14: Photography Tips

14.1 Recapturing the Essence of Angkor Wat

Angkor Wat, with its exquisite design and timeless beauty, provides numerous chances for photographers to capture the soul of this UNESCO World Heritage Site. Whether you're a seasoned expert or a novice enthusiast, these photography techniques can help you capture great images of Angkor Wat.

Photographic Techniques for Stunning Images

1. Golden Hours: - Photograph the delicate, warm colors of sunrise and sunset at Angkor Wat. The early morning and late afternoon light create a lovely environment that highlights the temple's unique intricacies. Use the 'golden hours' for optimal lighting conditions.

2. Silhouette shots: Experiment with silhouette photography at sunrise or sunset. Position yourself carefully to catch Angkor Wat's distinctive spires against a bright sky. Silhouettes bring drama and intrigue to your photographs.

3. Reflections:- Take advantage of the reflected ponds around Angkor Wat, especially in the early morning. Calm water surfaces produce wonderful reflections of the temple, increasing the visual impact of your photos.

4. Details and textures: Focus on the complex carvings, reliefs, and textures. Angkor Wat is embellished with numerous features that tell stories about ancient Khmer civilization. Use a macro lens or zoom to highlight the craftsmanship.

5. Wide-angle Views: Use wide-angle lenses to capture the magnificence of Angkor Wat. Stand back and capture the entire temple complex in your frame, highlighting its size and architectural magnificence.

6. People and Culture: - Include locals and visitors in your photos to lend a human touch. Candid photographs of people interacting with the temple, praying, or going about their daily lives provide cultural dimension to your photos.

7. Experiment with long exposure photographs at twilight. Smooth water surfaces or capture cloud movement to get ethereal and surreal effects.

8. HDR Photography: - High Dynamic Range (HDR) photography may capture delicate features of Angkor Wat while preserving balanced exposures, particularly in harsh lighting circumstances.

The Best Time and Angles for Photography

1. Sunrise at Angkor Wat: The iconic image of Angkor Wat at sunrise is one that must be captured. Arrive early to get a decent place. The sun rising behind the temple forms a striking silhouette, while the changing colors of the sky give a dynamic backdrop.

2. West-facing Angles for Sunset:- Photograph sunsets from Angkor Wat's west-facing angles. The warm glow of the evening sun bathes the temple in golden light, providing a unique yet equally captivating perspective.

3. Hidden Corners and Angles:- Explore beyond regularly photographed locales. Explore hidden corners and angles to snap one-of-a-kind images of Angkor Wat from unusual perspectives.

4. Consider going to the highest levels of Angkor Wat for panoramic vistas. This allows you to photograph the entire temple complex and surrounding area. Be aware of rules and operating hours.

5. Avoid crowds: Visit Angkor Wat during off-peak hours to reduce crowds in your photos. Midweek mornings and late evenings are generally quieter than peak visitor hours.

6. Seasonal Considerations: - Be mindful of seasonal changes in lighting and weather. The rainy season, which runs from May to October, provides unique picture opportunity with dramatic skies and rich flora, but be prepared for rain.

7. Check for unique events and festivals in Angkor Wat. These events offer cultural and dynamic photo opportunities, capturing the temple in a fresh light.

Practical Considerations:

1. Equipment: Bring a variety of lenses, including wide-angle and zoom lenses, to accommodate diverse views. A strong tripod is required for long exposure photographs and stabilizing your camera in low-light circumstances.

2. Camera Settings: Familiarize yourself with your camera's settings, such as aperture, shutter speed and ISO. Adjust the parameters based on the lighting and the style of shot you wish to create.

3. Respect local customs. Respect the temple's hallowed essence. Follow any guidelines issued by authorities and avoid disrupting religious events or rites.

4. Weather Preparedness: Siem Reap has a tropical climate, so be prepared for unexpected weather changes. Carry a rain cover for your camera and equipment, and shield yourself from the sun.

5. Editing and Post-Processing:- Try different post-processing techniques to improve your images. However, try for realism and avoid excessive editing to preserve Angkor Wat's natural beauty.

Angkor Wat's fascination stems not just from its historical significance, but also from its ageless beauty, which entices photographers to capture its essence. Armed with these photography suggestions, take a visual journey across Angkor Wat, capturing moments that embody the majesty and grandeur of this ancient wonder.

14.2 Gear and Equipment Recommendations.

Essential Photography Gear for Your Trip

Capturing the stunning majesty of Angkor Wat necessitates the proper photography equipment. Whether you're a professional photographer or a hobbyist trying to improve your skills, having the right equipment can help you make the most of your visit to this historic location.

Camera Body

Selecting the appropriate camera body is critical for producing high-quality photographs. Consider the choices below:

1. DSLR Cameras: Digital Single-Lens Reflex (DSLR) cameras provide high image quality and manual control. Photographers often employ popular models from brands such as Canon and Nikon.

2. Mirrorless Cameras: – Mirrorless cameras are tiny, lightweight, and gaining popularity. Mirrorless camera brands such as Sony, Fujifilm, and Panasonic are well-known for their innovative features and high image quality.

3. Point-and-Shoot Cameras: These cameras are ideal for casual photography. They are small, simple to use, yet still generate spectacular photographs.

Lenses.

With a range of lenses, you can capture diverse viewpoints and details:

1. Wide-Angle Lens: - Great for shooting broad landscapes and the grandeur of Angkor Wat. A 16-35mm or equivalent lens is recommended.

2. Zoom Lens: - A telephoto zoom lens (70-200mm) is ideal for catching temple details from a distance or highlighting specific elements.

3. Prime Lens: - A lens with a wide aperture (f/1.8 or lower) is ideal for low-light photography, such as dawn or sunset images.

4. Macro Lens: Use a macro lens to capture detailed carvings and details. This is especially beneficial for getting close-ups of the temple's architectural components.

Tripod.

A durable tripod is an essential gear for numerous sorts of photography.

1. Stability:- Use a tripod to stabilize your camera for lengthy exposures, low-light circumstances, or intricate photos.

2. Flexibility: - Choose a tripod with adjustable legs and ball head for versatile camera positioning.

Camera Bag.

1. Comfortable and spacious: Select a comfortable and capacious camera bag to transport your equipment. Make sure it allows simple access to your camera and lenses.

2. Weather Resistance: - For the tropical climate, choose a bag with weather-resistant characteristics to safeguard your gear from unexpected rain showers.

Accessories:

1. Extra Batteries and Memory Cards:

Bring extra camera batteries and memory cards to guarantee you never run out of power or storage capacity.

2. Lens Filters: - Polarizing and ND filters can enhance colors, minimize glare, and manage exposure under various lighting conditions.

3. Lens Hood: - A lens hood prevents lens flare and protects against direct sunlight.

4. Lens Cleaning Kit:- Keep a lens cleaning kit to keep your lenses dust and smudge-free.

5. Remote Shutter Release:- Capture long-exposure images without touching the camera, reducing camera shake.

Renting Gear locally

If you don't want to carry all of your gear or need something specific, renting equipment locally in Siem Reap is a convenient choice. Here's what you should know.

1. Local Rental stores: Siem Reap offers multiple camera rental stores offering a range of lenses, camera bodies, and accessories.

2. Costs: - Rental costs vary based on equipment and duration. Prices are often affordable, and renting locally allows you to avoid the inconvenience of transporting big equipment.

3. Check Availability: - Before arriving in Siem Reap, check with local rental shops to confirm they have the necessary items. Popular things could be in high demand.

4. Insurance: - Consider renting equipment with insurance coverage to prevent accidental damage or loss.

5. Test Equipment: - Upon renting, familiarize yourself with the equipment and confirm it works properly.

Having the proper equipment is vital for photographing the splendor of Angkor Wat. Choose a camera body and lenses that are appropriate for your photographic style, and don't overlook essential accessories such as a tripod and camera bag. If you want a smaller weight, consider renting gear locally in Siem Reap to fulfill your unique requirements throughout your photographic adventure through this historical wonder. With the correct tools, you can produce breathtaking visuals that capture the beauty of Angkor Wat.

Chapter 15: Conclusion

As we draw the curtain on this comprehensive guide to Angkor Wat, it's time for a brief recap of essential information, an encouraging note to share experiences, and heartfelt wishes for a memorable stay in this enchanting destination.

Recap of Essential Information

Throughout this guide, we've navigated the rich tapestry of Angkor Wat, uncovering its historical wonders, cultural gems, and practical tips for an immersive experience. From exploring iconic temples like Angkor Wat and Ta Prohm to delving into the vibrant local culture, each chapter has aimed to be your compass in this archaeological marvel.

Crucial aspects such as accommodation, transportation, dining, and entertainment have been meticulously addressed to ensure a seamless and enjoyable journey. Whether you're an avid history seeker, adventure enthusiast, or someone seeking tranquility, there's a facet of Angkor Wat waiting to be discovered by you.

Encouragement to Share Experiences and Recommendations

As you embark on your Angkor Wat adventure, we encourage you to share your experiences and recommendations. The magic of travel lies not only in personal exploration but in the shared stories that create a tapestry of collective memories. Engage with fellow travelers, exchange tips, and contribute to the collective wisdom that makes every journey richer.

Social media platforms, travel forums, and blogs are fantastic avenues to connect with like-minded individuals, seek advice, and inspire others to embark on their own Angkor Wat odyssey. Your unique perspective might be the catalyst for someone else's unforgettable experience.

Wishing You a Memorable and Enjoyable Stay in Angkor Wat!

As you set foot on the hallowed grounds of Angkor Wat, may your senses be awakened by the mystical aura that pervades this ancient city. May each temple reveal its secrets, each sunrise and sunset etch a lasting image in your memory, and each interaction with the locals add warmth to your journey.

Accommodation: Whether you choose the tranquility of boutique guesthouses, the uniqueness of unconventional stays, or the comfort of renowned hotels and resorts, may your lodgings be a sanctuary after a day of exploration.

Attractions: From the grandeur of Angkor Wat to the hidden gems like Preah Khan and the serene nature trails surrounding the temples, may every discovery leave you in awe of the architectural and natural marvels.

Activities: For the history seekers, adventure enthusiasts, wellness seekers, and everyone in between, may the activities you choose enrich your experience and create a tapestry of diverse memories.

Cultural Sensitivity: Respect for the local culture and customs is not just a tip but a pathway to meaningful connections. May your interactions be filled with mutual understanding and appreciation.

Safety and Well-being: Staying healthy, being environmentally conscious, and embracing responsible tourism practices contribute to the well-being of both travelers and the destination. May your journey be safe, enjoyable, and leave a positive impact on the places you visit.

In conclusion, Angkor Wat invites you to step into a realm where history whispers through ancient stones, nature unfolds its beauty, and the cultural vibrancy is a testament to the enduring spirit of Cambodia. May your stay be filled with moments that linger in your heart long after you've bid farewell to this extraordinary destination.

On behalf of this guide, we wish you a captivating, enlightening, and above all, an unforgettable stay in Angkor Wat. May your journey be as extraordinary as the temples that have withstood the test of time. Safe travels and may Angkor Wat weave its magic on your soul!

Made in the USA
Las Vegas, NV
25 November 2024

12609434R00153